W9-AKT-507

New Canaan Library

151 Main Street
New Canaan, CT 06840

(203)801-BOOK
www.newcanaanlibrary.org

DEMCO

FEB 03 2006

EASY FRENCH

Katie Daynes and Nicole Irving

Designed by Katarina Dragoslavić
Illustrated by Ann Johns

Edited by Jane Chisholm
Series designer: Russell Punter

Language consultant: Annie Turner
American editor: Carrie Seay
With thanks to Susan Meredith

Contents

J
448
D

About this book

This book provides an easy introduction to the French language. Each grammar page explains a particular topic, from nouns all the way to conditional sentences, with examples to show how French is used in everyday situations. The boxes shown below highlight different learning points, and there are recommended Web sites that give you further opportunity to put your French to the test.

This *Fais attention!* box means "Watch out!" It warns you of mistakes you might easily make and points out some of the differences between French and English grammar.

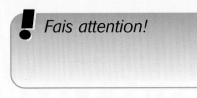

The *Learning tips* box tells you more about French grammar patterns and gives you clues to help you learn them more easily.

Learning tips

Each *Fast facts* box contains an extra gem of information. Impress your friends with your detailed knowledge of French!

Fast facts

When new verbs and tenses are introduced, they are clearly presented in a verb box, with the English translation alongside.

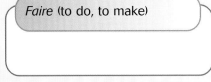

Faire (to do, to make)

Internet links

Look for little computer symbols in the right hand corner of the grammar pages. Here you'll find descriptions of useful Web sites where there are quizzes, games and tests to practice your French. To visit the recommended Web sites, go to the Usborne Quicklinks Web site at **www.usborne-quicklinks.com** and type in the key words "easy french".

The recommended Web sites have been selected by Usborne editors as suitable, in their opinion, for children, although no guarantees can be given and Usborne Publishing is not responsible for the accuracy or suitability of the information on any Web site other than its own. Before using the Internet, please read the Internet safety guidelines in Usborne Quicklinks. You can find more information about Usborne Internet links on pages 124-125 of this book.

The Camembert treasure: introduction

Throughout this book you can follow a story about a search for hidden treasure, using examples of the French grammar you'll be learning along the way. As new words crop up, they will be listed in the *New words* box. If you need extra help, there are translations of the speech bubbles on pages 100-111.

The main characters

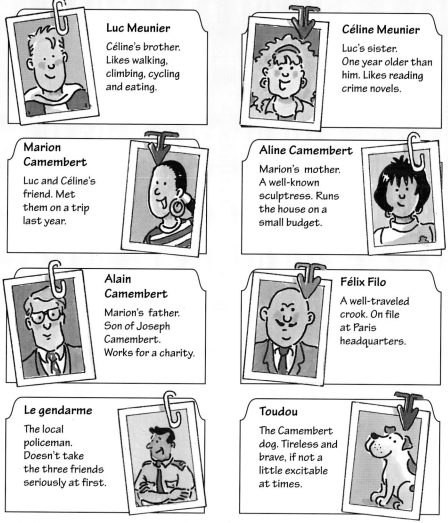

Luc Meunier
Céline's brother. Likes walking, climbing, cycling and eating.

Céline Meunier
Luc's sister. One year older than him. Likes reading crime novels.

Marion Camembert
Luc and Céline's friend. Met them on a trip last year.

Aline Camembert
Marion's mother. A well-known sculptress. Runs the house on a small budget.

Alain Camembert
Marion's father. Son of Joseph Camembert. Works for a charity.

Félix Filo
A well-traveled crook. On file at Paris headquarters.

Le gendarme
The local policeman. Doesn't take the three friends seriously at first.

Toudou
The Camembert dog. Tireless and brave, if not a little excitable at times.

Sometimes you will see this picture at the bottom of a page. It means there is a puzzle that needs to be solved. Look at the clues and try to figure out what Luc, Céline and Marion should do next.

Understanding grammar words

Grammar is the set of rules that summarizes how a language works. It is easier to learn how French works if you know a few grammar words. All the words you use when you speak or write can be split up into different types.

A **noun** is a word for a thing, an animal or a person, such as "box", "idea", "invention", "cat" or "woman". A noun is plural when you are talking about more than one, for example "boxes", "ideas" or "women".

cat

A **pronoun**, such as "he", "me" or "yours", is a word that stands in for a noun. If you say "The goat ate your clothes" and then, "He ate yours", you can see how "he" stands in for "goat" and "yours" stands in for "your clothes".

Is this **yours**?

An **adjective** is a word that describes something, usually a noun, for example "blue", as in "a blue jacket".

blue

Prepositions are link words such as "to", "at", "for", "near" and "under", as in "she is under the sea".

under the sea

A **verb** is an action word, such as "make", "play" or "eat", and also "have", "think" and "be". Verbs can change depending on who is doing the action, for example "I make", but "he makes". They have different **tenses** according to when the action takes place, for example "I make" but "I made". The infinitive form of the verb is its basic form: "to make", "to play" or "to eat". Dictionaries and word lists normally list verbs in this form.

to play soccer

An **adverb** is a word that gives extra information about an action. Many adverbs describe the action of a verb, for example "badly", as in "He plays tennis badly". Other adverbs describe when or where an action happens, for example "yesterday" or "here".

He plays **badly**.

Subject or object?

When used in a sentence, a noun or pronoun can have different parts to play. It is the **subject** when it is doing the action, for example "the dog" in "the dog barks" or "he" in "he barks". It is the **direct object** when it has the action done to it. For example, in the phrase "he brushes the dog", the dog is the direct object.

In the sentence "she gives money to the man", "she" is the subject, and "money" and "the man" are objects. "Money" is the direct object because it is the object that is being given. "The man" is the **indirect object** because the direct object is being given **to** him.

Accents

French has a few **accents**, which are special signs that you add over a vowel. The three French accents are ´ (acute), ` (grave) and ^ (circumflex). They most often go over an **e** and make it sound different. On other vowels, they do not change the sound, though the circumflex usually makes the sound longer.

You sometimes see ¨ over **e**, **i** or **u**. It means the vowel is said separately from the one before it (and **ë** is said like **ê**), for example in *Noël* and *aïe*. You can find out more about how to pronounce letters and words in French on page 98.

Laura passes the salad to David.
subject + verb + direct object + indirect object

Sarah drinks quietly.
subject + verb + adverb

Harry is bored.
subject + verb + adjective

Nouns

French nouns are either masculine [m] or feminine [f]. These are called genders. The article (the word for "the" or "a") varies according to the gender of a noun.

Saying "the"

• The masculine word for "the" is *le*.
• The feminine word for "the" is *la*.
• With nouns beginning with a vowel and some nouns beginning with *h*, both *le* and *la* become *l'*.
• The plural word for "the" is *les* for all nouns.

Masculine or feminine?

For a few nouns the gender is as you might expect:

e.g. *l'homme* (man) is masculine.

e.g. *la femme* (woman) is feminine.

For most nouns the gender seems random, so you just have to learn it:

le cinéma   *la montagne*
(movie theatre)   (mountain)

Some nouns have two forms:

l'amie [f]   *l'ami* [m]   (friend)

Saying "a"

• The masculine word for "a" is *un*.
• The feminine word for "a" is *une*.
• In English the plural of "a" is "some" and in French the word used is *des*.

Some examples:

un aéroport (airport)   *une route* (road)

un hôtel (hotel)   *une maison* (house)

8

Making plurals

For most French plurals you simply add *s* on the end of the noun:

le village - *les villages*
(village)
un ordinateur - *des ordinateurs*
(computer)

For the plural of nouns ending in *-au* or *-eau*, you add *x*:
le château - *les châteaux*
(castle)

Learning tips

• Try to learn nouns with *le* or *la* in front of them so that you remember their gender.

• Learn nouns with *un* or *une* in front of them if they begin with a vowel or *h*.

• Many nouns ending in *e* are feminine, so try guessing the gender if you can't remember it.

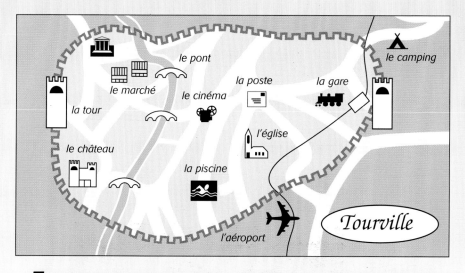

le pont
le camping
la poste
la gare
le marché
le cinéma
la tour
l'église
le château
la piscine
l'aéroport
Tourville

! *Fais attention! (Watch out!)*

In French you don't always use articles in the same way as you do in English.

• English often leaves out "some" where French uses *des*, such as *des montagnes* (mountains).

• When talking about a noun in a general way, in French you use an article but in English you

don't, such as *J'aime le thé* (I like tea) or *J'étudie la géographie* (I study geography).

• When stating someone's profession, English uses an article but French doesn't:
e.g. *Je suis mécanicien.*
(I'm **a** mechanic.)
Mon père est professeur.
(My father is **a** teacher.)

The Camembert treasure: chapter 1

Luc and his sister Céline are flying to Tourville from Paris to spend some time with their friend Marion Camembert...

New words

l'aéroport [m]	airport
le bonbon	candy
la carte	map
la côte	coast
le lac	lake
la maison	house
la montagne	mountain
le pont	bridge
le port	port
la rivière	river
la tour	tower
le village	village
la ville	town
c'est	it/this/that is
il y a	there is/are
aussi	too, also
deux	two
et	and
oui	yes
regarde!	look!
qu'est-ce que c'est?	what is it/this/that?
super	great
voilà	there is/are
voici	here is/are

...et les deux tours.

Oh, voilà l'aéroport.

Qu'est-ce que c'est, Céline?

Super! Des bonbons.

C'est la carte.

Et voici la maison Camembert.

Oui, voilà la maison.

la maison Camembert

As Luc and Céline look at the map on their way in to land, the man sitting behind them is also studying it closely. He too is working out the best way to get to the Camembert house.

Adjectives

Most French adjectives come after the noun, unlike English adjectives, and they almost all change if the noun is feminine or plural. This is known as "agreeing".

Making adjectives agree

You can make most adjectives agree with feminine nouns by adding an **e**, e.g. *vert* (green) becomes *verte*. Some adjectives, such as *jaune*, already end in **e** and don't change. Others have irregular endings.

la valise verte
(the green suitcase)

le sac noir
(the black bag)

la tente jaune
(the yellow tent)

With plural masculine nouns, or a group of masculine and feminine nouns, you add **s** to the adjective, e.g. *les chapeaux bleus* (blue hats). With plural feminine nouns, add **es**.

les vacances parfaites
(perfect vacation)

Before the noun?

A few French adjectives come before the noun. Here is a list of them. The letters in brackets show what to add to make the feminine version of the adjective. If there are two masculine versions, the second is to use with nouns beginning with a vowel or an *h*, e.g. *le vieil homme* (the old man).

beau/bel (belle)	beautiful
bon(ne)	good
gentil(le)	nice, kind
grand(e)	big, tall
gros(se)	big, fat
haut(e)	high
jeune	young
joli(e)	pretty
long(ue)	long
mauvais(e)	bad
petit(e)	small, little
vieux/vieil (vieille)	old

Bon voyage! (Have a good journey!)

un bel endroit (a beautiful place)

la longue route (the long road)

Some adjectives never change to agree with the noun they are with: e.g. *marron* (brown), *argent* (silver).

First verbs

French verbs seem more complicated than English verbs because there are lots of different patterns to learn. There are several groups of "regular" verbs which follow the same pattern as the verbs in their own group. Then there are "irregular" verbs that have their own unique pattern. Before the verb, you put either a subject noun (e.g. the dog, Pierre, Mom, etc.) or a pronoun (e.g. I, you, he, etc.).

I, you, he, she, etc.

I - *je* (or *j'* in front of vowels)

you - *tu* or *vous*
• Use *tu* when talking to a friend, or someone your own age or younger.
• Use *vous* when talking to more than one person. *Vous* is also the polite form, for addressing an older person or someone you don't know very well.

he - *il* **she** - *elle* **it** - *il* or *elle*
• There is no word for it, so use *il* for masculine [m] nouns and *elle* for feminine [f] nouns.

we - *nous* or *on*
• *On* can also be translated as "one" or sometimes "you". It is very common in French.

they - *ils* [m] or *elles* [f]
• When referring to a mixture of masculine and feminine things, or a mixed group of people, use *ils*.

Cette île a une jolie plage.
(This island has a pretty beach.)

L'herbe est verte. (The grass is green.)

Two useful irregular verbs

Avoir (to have)

j'ai	I have
tu as	you have
il/elle a	he/she/it has
nous avons	we have
vous avez	you have
ils/elles ont	they have

Être (to be)

je suis	I am
tu es	you are
il/elle est	he/she/it is
nous sommes	we are
vous êtes	you are
ils/elles sont	they are

Learning tip

In the word lists of this book, irregular verbs are marked by an asterisk *.

L'eau est claire. (The water is clear.)

Le sable est jaune.
(The sand is yellow.)

The Camembert treasure: chapter 2

Luc and Céline have landed at the airport, but there seems to be some confusion in the baggage claim area...

New words

le sac	bag
le sac à dos	backpack
la sortie	exit, way out
la tente	tent
la valise	suitcase
à	at, to, in
allô	hello (on phone)
bien	well
bleu(e)	blue
ça va	(it's) all right
fatigué(e)	tired
gentil(le)	kind
grand(e)	big, large, tall
gris(e)	gray
Mademoiselle	Miss
mais	but
merci	thank you
mon, ma, mes[1]	my
noir(e)	black
non	no
pardon	sorry, excuse me
petit(e)	small
rouge	red
son, sa, ses[1]	his/her/its
ton, ta, tes[1]	your
vert(e)	green
votre[1]	your

[1]For more information about this kind of adjective, go to page 21.

Making the present tense

There are two main groups of French verbs that follow regular patterns. They are called ER verbs and IR verbs, because their infinitives (e.g. to walk, to choose, etc.) end in -er or -ir. To make the present tense of these verbs, you take off the -er/-ir and add a special set of endings.

ER verbs

The infinitive of the verb "to walk" is *marcher*. Take off the -er and you are left with the stem, *march-*. Now you can add the present tense endings:

Marcher (to walk)

je march**e**	I walk (am walking)
tu march**es**	you walk
il/elle march**e**	he/she/it walks
nous march**ons**	we walk
vous march**ez**	you walk
ils/elles march**ent**	they walk

Here are some more ER verbs that follow the same pattern as *marcher*:

aimer	to like
briller	to shine
chanter	to sing
chercher	to look for
continuer	to continue
manger	to eat
porter	to carry, to wear
visiter	to visit

Fais attention!

In French, you don't distinguish between the two English present tenses ("I walk" and "I am walking") so *je marche* can mean either.

IR verbs

The infinitive of the verb "to choose" is *choisir*. Take off the -ir and you are left with the stem, *chois-*. IR verbs have a different set of endings from ER verbs.

Choisir (to choose)

je chois**is**	I choose (am choosing)
tu chois**is**	you choose
il/elle chois**it**	he/she/it chooses
nous chois**issons**	we choose
vous chois**issez**	you choose
ils/elles chois**issent**	they choose

Other verbs that follow the same pattern as *choisir* include:

bâtir	to build
finir	to finish
grandir	to grow
réfléchir	to think, to reflect
saisir	to seize

Learning tips

• Learn the endings separately, then you can add them to any regular verb.

• In spoken French, -e, -es and -ent endings all sound the same, and -is sounds like -it. Practice saying the words out loud to help you learn them.

What would you like?

The French for "to want" is *vouloir*. As *vouloir* doesn't follow a pattern, you must learn it separately.

Vouloir (to want)

je veux	I want (am wanting)
tu veux	you want
il/elle veut	he/she/it wants
nous voulons	we want
vous voulez	you want
ils/elles veulent	they want

I want to...

You can use *vouloir* with another verb to say what you want to do. Put the second verb in the infinitive form:
e.g. *Je veux visiter la Tour Eiffel.*
(I want to visit the Eiffel Tower.)

Being polite

When you want to ask for something politely, you use *vouloir* in a special tense (the conditional) and say:
je voudrais (I would like).

You can use *je voudrais* + infinitive to say what you would like to do.
e.g. *Je voudrais aller à la piscine.*
(I'd like to go to the swimming pool.)

Saying please

There are two ways of saying "please" in French. You either say:
s'il te plaît when talking to someone you know well,
OR
s'il vous plaît when talking to someone you don't know very well, or when addressing more than one person.

17

The Camembert treasure: chapter 3

Luc and Céline have managed to collect their bags from the airport and are now on their way to Marion's house. They stop at a café for a rest...

A man walking past Céline drops a letter. By the time she has picked it up for him, he has driven away.

Oh!

Nous voulons louer des vélos.

When she looks at the letter, she sees it's very strange. It's written to a son named Joseph and signed Clément Camembert...

Une île déserte,
1948

Mon cher fils Joseph,

Je suis un vieil homme. Je suis seul sur mon île déserte et ma maison près de Tourville est vide. J'ai un secret. Je suis très riche.

Maintenant mon trésor est ton trésor. Ma maison cache le premier indice. D'abord tu cherches les deux bateaux.

Adieu,
Clément Camembert

New words

l'appareil-photo [m]	camera
le bateau(x)¹	boat, ship
le coca	Coke
le fils	son
l'homme [m]	man
l'indice [m]	clue
la limonade	lemonade
l'oiseau(x) [m]	bird
le paysage	countryside
le secret	secret
le soleil	sun
la table	table
le trésor	treasure
le vélo	bike
briller	to shine
cacher	to hide
chanter	to sing
chercher	to look (for)
continuer	to continue
louer	to rent
payer	to pay
regarder	to look (at)
à l'ombre	in the shade
adieu	farewell
cher (chère)	dear
d'abord	first of all
désert(e)	deserted
deux	two
facile	easy
glacé(e)	ice-cold
lentement	slowly
maintenant	now
moi	me
riche	rich
premier, première	first
seul(e)	alone, only
s'il vous plaît	please
tout droit	straight ahead

¹If a noun has an irregular plural ending, it will be noted in brackets after the noun, e.g. the plural of le bateau(x) is les bateaux.

19

Whose is it?

In French, to say something belongs to someone, you use *de* (of). So "Paul's sweater" is, word for word, "the sweater of Paul" - *le pull de Paul*. To say "It's Paul's", you use *à* (which means "at" or "to"). So the answer to "Whose sweater is it?" is *C'est* or *Il est* (because *le pull* is masculine) *à Paul*.

Using *de*

When you use *de* with a feminine noun, such as "the girl", you just add *la fille*. So "the girl's boots" is *les bottes de la fille*.

But with masculine and plural nouns, when *de* is followed by *le* or *les*, it changes to make a new word:
de + le = du, *de + les = des*.

Using *à*

À also changes when you join it to *le* and *les*, but not when it comes before *la*. So, in answer to the question "Whose is it?" (*C'est à qui?*), you say *C'est à la fille*, but *C'est au garçon* and *C'est aux filles*.

Appartenir *à* (to belong to)

Another way to say that something belongs to someone is to use the verb *appartenir* (to belong). It follows the pattern of the useful irregular verb *tenir* shown below. Just put *appar-* in front of the form you need:
e.g. *il appartient à...* (it belongs to...)

Tenir (to hold)

je tiens	I hold (am holding)
tu tiens	you hold
il/elle tient	he/she/it holds
nous tenons	we hold
vous tenez	you hold
ils/elles tiennent	they hold

This, these

French has different words for "this" and "these", depending on the gender of the noun. With masculine nouns, you say *ce* (or *cet* if the noun begins with a vowel or *h*). With feminine nouns, you say *cette* and with plural nouns, *ces* (these).

💭 *Learning tip*

Remember these patterns:

de + le = du   *à + le = au*
de + les = des   *à + les = aux*

Fast facts

the...	this...
le paysage	ce paysage
l'hôtel	cet hôtel
la chaussure	cette chaussure
les bottes	ces bottes

My, your, his, her...

In French, the words for my, your, his, etc. are a special kind of adjective and must agree with the noun they refer to.
Here are the different forms:

	[m]	[f]	[pl]
my	*mon*	*ma*	*mes*
your	*ton*	*ta*	*tes*
his/her /its	*son*	*sa*	*ses*
our	*notre*	*notre*	*nos*
your	*votre*	*votre*	*vos*
their	*leur*	*leur*	*leurs*

e.g. *J'aime **ta** robe et **son** jean.*
(I like your dress and his/her jeans.)

Les vêtements

les baskets [f]	tennis shoes
les bottes [f]	boots
la ceinture	belt
le chapeau(x)	hat
la chaussette	sock
la chaussure	shoe
la chemise	shirt
le collant	tights
le costume	suit
le jean[1]	jeans
la jupe	skirt
les lunettes [f]	glasses
le pantalon[1]	pants
le pull	sweater
la robe	dress
le short[1]	shorts
le sweat-shirt	sweatshirt
le tee-shirt	T-shirt
la veste	jacket
les vêtements [m]	clothes

[1]In French, the words for pants, jeans and shorts are singular if you are talking about one pair.

Nous portons nos vêtements neufs.
We're wearing our new clothes.

mon tee-shirt

mon pull

ma chemise

mon jean

mon pantalon

mes baskets

mes chaussures

21

The Camembert treasure: chapter 4

Luc and Céline arrive at the Camembert house, where they are shown lots of interesting things and meet a very destructive goat in the garden. How silly of them to leave their bags on the steps outside...

New words

l'ami [m]	friend
l'atelier [m]	studio
la chambre	(bed)room
le chat	cat
la chèvre	goat
le chien	dog
le frère	brother
le grand-père	grandfather
les jumelles [f]	binoculars
le locataire	roomer
les lunettes [f]	glasses
la mère	mother
les parents [m]	parents
la pièce	room
le portrait	portrait
le tableau(x)	painting
les voisins	neighbors
je m'appelle	my name is
il s'appelle	his/its name is
à qui?	whose?
	to who(m)?
bonjour	hello
préféré(e)	favorite

23

Telling people what to do

There are several ways to tell someone what to do in French. You can use the imperative of the verb (Wait! Go! Stop!), or you can use "must" or "have to", as in "You must clean your room."

Making the imperative

To make the imperative in French, you normally use the verb's present tense in the *tu* or *vous* form, leaving out the words *tu* and *vous*. With ER verbs you also drop the *-s* from the end of the *tu* form.

Tu marches becomes ***Marche!*** (Walk!)

Useful imperatives

Here is a list of imperatives that are used very often. They come from irregular verbs.

tu form	*vous* form	
va	allez	go!
		(from *aller*)
sois	soyez	be!
		(from *être*)
fais	faites	do!
		(from *faire*)
prends	prenez	take!
		(from *prendre*)
viens	venez	come!
		(from *venir*)
suis	suivez	follow!
		(from *suivre*)

Saying "must"

Devoir (to have to, must) followed by an infinitive is a common way of saying what someone must do. To say "we must" you often use **on doit**, e.g. *On doit payer.* (One/we must pay.)

Devoir (to have to, must)

je dois	I must
tu dois	you must
il/elle/on doit	he/she/it/ one must
nous devons	we must
vous devez	you must
ils/elles doivent	they must

Vous devez acheter ça. You must buy this.

Fast facts

You can also make an imperative with the *nous* form, simply by dropping the *nous*. The equivalent in English is to add "let's" before the verb:

e.g. *Commençons!* (Let's start!)

Giving directions

The imperative is very useful for giving and understanding directions. Here is a list of direction words:

le carrefour	intersection
le chemin	path, lane, way
les feux [m]	traffic lights
le passage piétons	pedestrian crossing
la place	square
la (grande) route	(main) road
la rue	street
aller*	to go
continuer	to continue
prendre*	to take
suivre*	to follow
tourner	to turn
traverser	to cross
venir*	to come
premier (première)	first
deuxième	second
troisième	third
quatrième	fourth
tout droit	straight ahead
à gauche	(to/on the) left
à droite	(to/on the) right

Using *il faut*

The French verb *falloir* means "to be necessary" and the *il* form - ***il faut*** - is very common in French. It can be followed by an infinitive to mean "you must", in the general sense of "people have to" or "one must". You can also use it instead of *nous devons* or *on doit* for "we must".

Il faut réserver. You must book.

! *Fais attention!*

Some verbs, called reflexive verbs (see page 44), have an extra pronoun, e.g. *se laver* (to wash oneself). In the imperative, the pronouns ***-toi***, ***-nous*** or ***-vous*** come after the verb, for example:
tu form: *lave-toi!* (wash!)
nous form: *lavons-nous!* (let's wash!)
vous form: *lavez-vous!* (wash!)

Des amis jouent au soleil.
(Some friends are playing in the sun.)

Passe le ballon!
Pass the ball!

Va à gauche!
Go left!

Il faut gagner!
We must win!

The Camembert treasure: chapter 5

The three friends are doing battle with Mangetout, the neighbor's goat. They're having a tough time getting the animal back where it belongs.

That chore done, the three friends decide to visit an old church nearby. They go off on their bicycles, leaving the house unattended...

Unknown to them, an unwelcome visitor arrives.

New words

la barrière	gate
la corde	rope
la grotte	cave
la lime	nail file
la serrure	lock
devoir*	to have to
faire* attention	to watch out, to be careful
faire* des courses	to do some shopping
fermer	to close, to shut
lancer	to throw
prendre*	to take
rester	to stay, to remain
se dépêcher	to hurry (up)
se taire*	to be quiet
tirer	to pull
trouver	to find
venir*	to come
visiter	to visit
à tout à l'heure	see you later
attention!	watch out!
ce, c'	this/that/it
doucement	slowly
ici	here
Madame	Mrs, Madam
sage	well behaved
tout	everything
tranquille	quiet, calm
vite	quickly, fast

27

Asking questions

There are three different ways to ask questions in French and many question words - such as when, where, why - that can be added to the sentence.

Add a question mark

The easiest way to ask a question is simply to change the tone of your voice. In written French you show this change by putting a question mark (?) at the end of the sentence.

Vous avez des croissants?
Do you have any croissants?

Add *est-ce-que*

Another easy way to ask questions is to put **est-ce que** at the start of the sentence:

e.g. *Est-ce que vous avez une chambre libre ce soir?*
(Do you have a room free tonight?)

Make an inversion

Often you make a sentence into a question by switching out the subject and the verb. This is called an inversion. When the sentence is a statement, the order is subject + verb.
With an inversion, this becomes verb + subject. So *Tu as un frère* (You have a brother) becomes *As-tu un frère?* (Do you have a brother?)

Question words

combien (de)?	how much/many?
comment?	how?
où?	where?
pourquoi?	why?
quand?	when?
que?	what?
quel(le)[1]*?*	which?/what?
qui?	who?

[1]**Quel** changes like an adjective to agree with the noun that follows. The feminine version of *quel* is **quelle** and the plural is **quels** or **quelles**:
e.g. *Quelle glace veux-tu?*
(Which ice-cream do you want?)

À quelle heure part le train?
When does the train leave?

Pourquoi il est en retard?
Why is it late?

How to use question words

Question words usually go at the beginning of the sentence. So, to ask "Where are you?" you can either say: *Où tu es?*
Où est-ce que tu es? or *Où es-tu?*

If the subject is *je* (I), then it is better to avoid a word inversion because it can sound awkward.

28

Can I? May I?

The irregular French verb *pouvoir* can be translated as "to be able to", "can" or "may". You often use this verb with another verb in the infinitive to ask permission to do something, such as:

Est-ce que je peux regarder? (May I look?)
Est-ce que mon chien peut entrer? (Can my dog come in?)

Pouvoir (can, may)

je peux	I can/I may
tu peux	you can
il/elle peut	he/she/it can
nous pouvons	we can
vous pouvez	you can
ils/elles peuvent	they can

Pouvoir also has an irregular *je* form - *puis* - that is only used in inversions and is very polite: e.g. **Puis-je** *prendre une photo?* (May I take a photo?)

Fast facts

• *Quel* + noun can also be used in exclamations: e.g. *Quelle surprise!* (What a surprise!)

• *Pouvoir* has a special *je* form for questions: *puis-je?*

Faire les courses

la boulangerie	bakery
la fraise	strawberry
le gâteau(x)	cake
la glace	ice-cream
le kilo (followed by *de/d'* + noun)	kilo (of)
le parfum	flavor, perfume
le panier	basket
la pharmacie	pharmacy
la pomme	apple
l'orange [f]	orange
le supermarché	supermarket
coûter	to cost
expliquer	to explain
faire* les courses	to go shopping
fermer	to close
goûter	to taste
porter	to carry, to wear

Combien coûtent les chaussures?
How much do these shoes cost?

Puis-je voir ce tee-shirt là?
May I see that t-shirt?

29

The Camembert treasure: chapter 6

Marion's mother, Aline, is doing her grocery shopping...

Meanwhile, Luc, Céline and Marion have arrived at the church. While they're resting, Céline remembers the letter that the man dropped at the café...

Marion knows that Clément was her great-grandfather. After studying his letter to his son Joseph, she realizes that it is the start of a trail of clues leading to hidden treasure.

First they will need to go back to the house to look at the two old pictures of ships...

New words

la blague	joke
la chasse au trésor	treasure hunt
le crabe	crab
la lettre	letter
le magicien	magician
la pharmacie	pharmacy
ce sont	they are
expliquer	to explain
malade	ill
Monsieur or M.	Mr.
parce que	because
vrai(e)	true

31

Negatives

To make a sentence negative, you put *ne* and *pas* on either side of the verb, so that *je pense* (I think) becomes *je ne pense pas* (I don't think). There are other negative words that can be used with *ne*, which mean "never", "nobody", or "nothing". The word order is the same, unless the negative word becomes the subject of the sentence.

Useful negative words

ne...jamais (never), as in:
Il ne mange jamais.
(He never eats.)

ne...personne (nobody, not anybody), as in:
Ils ne trouvent personne.
(They can't find anybody.)

ne...rien (nothing, not anything), as in:
Je ne veux rien.
(I don't want anything.)

Je suis désolé mais je ne peux pas la réparer.
I'm sorry but I can't repair it.

Making contractions

When we shorten a word or phrase and add an apostrophe (') to show where the letters are missing, it is called a contraction (don't, can't, etc.). In French, *ne*, *de* and *je* contract before a vowel. They lose their -e and become *n'*, *d'* and *j'*.

e.g. *Je n'ai pas d'oranges.*
(I don't have any oranges.)

Ne...pas de

When *ne...pas* is used with an object, you add *de* before the noun, or *d'* if the noun begins with a vowel or *h*. You also leave out the word for "the":

e.g. *Il n'a pas de pain.*
(He doesn't have any bread.)

Nothing and nobody

In French, if "nothing" or "nobody" is the subject of the sentence then the order of the sentence changes. The new order is:
Rien or *personne* + *ne* + verb
e.g. *Rien ne change.*
(Nothing changes.)

Personne ne me comprend!
Nobody understands me!

Learning tips

The French singer Edith Piaf was famous for the song *Je ne regrette rien* (I don't regret anything). Learning songs and poems can be a great way to remember French grammar.

Saying that you know

French uses two different verbs to talk about "what" and "who" you know. To say that you know how to do something (e.g. I know how to swim), you use *savoir*. To say that you know, or are acquainted with, someone or somewhere, you use *connaître*. Both verbs are irregular.

Savoir (to know, to know how to)

je sais	I know
tu sais	you know
il/elle sait	he/she/it knows
nous savons	we know
vous savez	you know
ils/elles savent	they know

Fast facts

• *Savoir* means to know how to. In English we say someone has "savoir-faire", meaning they know how to do things.

• *Connaître* means to know a person or a place.

Connaître (to know, to be acquainted with)

je connais	I know
tu connais	you know
il/elle connaît	he/she/it knows
nous connaissons	we know
vous connaissez	you know
ils/elles connaissent	they know

Likes and dislikes

The best way to say "I like" is *j'aime*, from the verb *aimer* (to like, to love). This follows the regular ER pattern (see page 16). You often add *bien* (well) after it when all you mean is "to like". This is because, on its own, *aimer* can mean "to love", especially when you are talking about people:

e.g. *J'aime bien les bijoux.*
(I like jewelry.)
J'aime mon mari.
(I love my husband.)

To say "I don't like" you use the negative form of *aimer* -
je n'aime pas.

Qui gagne?
Who's winning?

Je ne sais pas.
I don't know.

Ce n'est pas possible!
That's not possible!

The Camembert treasure: chapter 7

Aline arrives home with her groceries. She starts cooking without realizing there's someone in the house or, to be more precise, someone in her studio...

Marion, Luc and Céline arrive home and head straight for the studio and the two paintings. The burglar makes a hasty retreat...

New words

l'aspirine [f]	aspirin
la porte	door
le sparadrap	adhesive bandage
le voleur	burglar
aboyer	to bark
arriver	to arrive, to happen
dîner	to have supper
bonsoir	good evening
la clé	key
chéri [m], *chérie* [f]	darling, dear
dans	in
dehors	outside
exactement	exactly
fermé(e) à clé	locked
fort	loud(ly)
jamais	never
(ne...jamais)	(not...ever)
là	there
pareil(le)	(the) same
par ici	this way
personne	nobody
(ne...personne)	(not...anybody)
salut	hi, hello, bye
si	so
tout le monde	everybody

The first clue

Six missing items in the second picture are enough to tell the three friends where the next clue must be. They decide to go there the next day.

Picture one

Picture two

Can you spot which six items are missing in the second picture?
(The same items have already appeared in the story, on a sign over a door...)

Coming and going

There is a very useful group of irregular verbs, describing coming and going, that does not follow the regular ER and IR patterns mentioned on page 16. You can read about them on these two pages. They are best learned one by one.

Coming

In French, the verb "to come" is *venir*. It is irregular and follows a different pattern from *choisir*. However, there are a couple of verbs which share its pattern: *revenir* (to come back) and *devenir* (to become).

Venir (to come)	
je viens	I come (am coming)
tu viens	you come
il/elle vient	he/she/it comes
nous venons	we come
vous venez	you come
ils/elles viennent	they come

A special use of *venir*

Venir, followed by *de* and an infinitive, is used like a past tense, and means "to have just done something".

Je viens de faire mes cheveux.
I've just done my hair.

Going somewhere

To talk about going **to** a place, you use the irregular verb *aller*.

Aller (to go)	
je vais	I go (am going)
tu vas	you go
il/elle va	he/she/it goes
nous allons	we go
vous allez	you go
ils/elles vont	they go

Tu vas dans la mauvaise direction!
You're going the wrong way!

A special use of *aller*

The verb *aller*, followed by an infinitive, can be used as a kind of future tense. It means "going to":

e.g. *Je vais parler à Marion.*
(I'm going to speak to Marion.)

You can find out more about describing future events on page 77.

Leaving and going out

To talk about leaving or going **away** from a place, you use the verb *partir* (to go, to leave):
e.g. *Je pars de la maison.*
(I'm leaving the house.)

Partir shares its pattern with a few other verbs, including *sortir* (to go out). For a list of common irregular verbs, go to pages 112-115.

Partir (to go (away), to leave)	
je pars	I leave (am leaving)
tu pars	you leave
il/elle part	he/she/it leaves
nous partons	we leave
vous partez	you leave
ils/elles partent	they leave

Fast facts

To encourage a friend by saying "go on!" or "do it!" you use the verb *aller* with the pronoun *y* and say *Vas-y!*
You can also use the *nous* form and say *Allons-y!* (Let's go!)

Taking and eating

The French word for "to take" is *prendre*. It can be used to talk about how you travel:

e.g. *Ils prennent l'autobus.*
(They're going by bus.)

It can also be used to talk about food and drink. The equivalent in English would be "to have":

e.g. *Je prends du thé.*
(I'm having some tea.)

Prendre (to take)	
je prends	I take (am taking)
tu prends	you take
il/elle prend	he/she/it takes
nous prenons	we take
vous prenez	you take
ils/elles prennent	they take

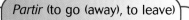

Je vais à Paris demain!
I'm going to Paris tomorrow!

Génial! Tu prends l'avion où le train?
Cool! By plane or by train?

The Camembert treasure: chapter 8

The next day, Luc, Céline and Marion have arrived at the *Magician's Inn*, in search of the next clue. Marion has her camera with her. But finding what they're looking for isn't easy with all those people around, and unknown to the three friends they are being watched...

New words

les frites [f]	French fries
le fromage	cheese
le gosse	kid
le journal	newspaper
le légume	vegetable
la photo	photo
le soir	evening
la soupe	soup
le supermarché	supermarket
le train	train
adorer	to adore, to love
agacer	to annoy/bother
apporter	to bring
*apprendre**	to learn
*comprendre**	to understand
exagérer	to exaggerate
*lire**	to read
manger	to eat
*partir**	to leave
*sentir**	to feel, to smell
*sortir**	to go out
à quelle heure?	what time?
bon(ne)	good, right, nice
bientôt	soon
ça suffit	that's enough
et puis	and then/also
prochain(e)	next
tout de suite	right away

39

Prepositions

Prepositions are words like "in", "on" or "of". Most French prepositions are easy to use, for example:
Ton pull est sous la table. (Your sweater is under the table.)

Common prepositions

à	at, to
à côté de	next to
après	after
à travers	through
avant	before
avec	with
chez X	at the house of X, at X's
contre	against
dans	in, into
de	of, from
derrière	behind
devant	in front of
en	in (a language, color, season or month), made of
en face de	opposite
entre	between
hors de	out of
jusqu'à	as far as, until
loin de	far from
par	by, through
pour	for
(tout) près de	(very) near to
sous	under
sur	on, onto
vers	toward

Prepositions and places

In French, to say "from" and "to" you normally use *de* and *à*:
e.g. *Je viens de France.*
(I come **from** France.)
e.g. *Je vais à Nice.*
(I'm going **to** Nice.)

To say that you are going **to**, or that you are **in** a certain country, you use *en* with feminine country names and *au* with masculine country names:
e.g. *Je suis en Italie.* (I'm **in** Italy.)

A few masculine countries, such as *les États-Unis* (the US) and *les Pays Bas* (the Netherlands), are plural and use *aux*:
e.g. *Je vais aux États-Unis.*
(I'm going **to** the US.)

Je veux aller à Paris.
I want to go to Paris.

! *Fais attention!*

In French you don't always use the same preposition as in English:
e.g. *Je suis **dans** le train.*
(I'm **on** the train.)
Je regarde le sport à la télé.
(I watch sports **on** TV.)

Learning tips

When *de* and *à* come at the end of a longer preposition (e.g. *loin de, jusqu'à*), they join together with *le* and *les*:

de + le = du	*à + le = au*
de + les = des	*à + les = aux*

Internet link: go to **www.usborne-quicklinks.com** for a link to a Web site where you can find out more about French prepositions and place names.

Where do you live?

The French word *habiter* means "to live in", so you don't need to add a preposition after it. In answer to the question *Où habites-tu?* (Where do you live?), you can say *J'habite la France* (I live in France) or *J'habite Paris* (I live in Paris), without using a preposition.

Using *chez*

The French for "at my home" or "at mine" is *chez moi*. *Chez* is a preposition and *moi* is a pronoun meaning "me". You can use *chez* with other pronouns, such as *chez elle* (at her house) and *chez eux* (at their house). For more on these pronouns, go to page 52.

Chez can also be used with people's names:
e.g. *Je vais chez Paul demain.*
(I'm going to Paul's tomorrow.)

or with people's professions:
e.g. *J'achète le pain chez le boulanger.*
(I buy bread at the bakery.)

Some country names

l'Allemagne [f]	Germany
l'Angleterre [f]	England
l'Australie [f]	Australia
l'Autriche [f]	Austria
l'Écosse [f]	Scotland
l'Espagne [f]	Spain
les États-Unis [m]	United States
la France	France
l'Irlande [f]	Ireland
l'Italie [f]	Italy
le Japon	Japan
le Pays de Galles	Wales

The continents

l'Amérique [f] *du Nord*
North America

l'Europe [f]
Europe

l'Asie [f]
Asia

l'Amérique [f] *du Sud*
South America

l'Afrique [f]
Africa

l'Australasie [f]
Australasia

Deux amies sont assises sur le sable au bord de la mer.
Two friends are sitting on the sand by the sea.

Brigitte est sous le parasol.
Brigitte is under the parasol.

Marie est à côté d'elle.
Marie is next to her.

41

The Camembert treasure: chapter 9

Outside the inn, Céline spots the man who has been following them. He is on his way out. Luc, Céline and Marion realize they have seen him before. He too must be after the treasure.

They have to lose him quickly, so they head for the harbor.

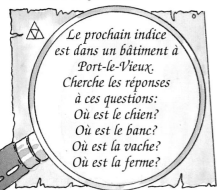

Allons chez mon copain, Jérôme. Il habite en face de la gare.

Oui, j'ai une loupe. Elle est sur la table dans le grenier.

New words

l'arbre [m]	tree
le banc	bench
le bâtiment	building
la colline	hill
le copain, la copine	mate, good friend
l'école [f]	school
l'église [f]	church
la femme	woman
la fenêtre	window
la ferme	farm
le filet	net
la fontaine	fountain
le grenier	attic
le jardin	garden/backyard
la loupe	magnifying glass
le/la/les même(s)	the same
le mot	word, note
le quai	quay, platform
la question	question
la réponse	answer
la vache	cow
habiter	to live
poser	to place
à la maison	(at) home
chauve	bald

Using the magnifying glass, Luc, Marion and Céline look at the note that Luc found at the inn. At first it is very puzzling, but with the help of Marion's photograph of the painted seat at the inn, they work out where to go next.

Le prochain indice est dans un bâtiment à Port-le-Vieux. Cherche les réponses à ces questions: Où est le chien? Où est le banc? Où est la vache? Où est la ferme?

Can you figure out where the three friends must go next? (Try and find a building on this page which matches the answers to Clément Camembert's questions. The first answer is *sous l'arbre.*)

Reflexive verbs

Reflexive verbs are verbs which include a pronoun, such as *me* (myself) and *te* (yourself). The pronoun "reflects back" the subject of the verb, which means that the subject and the object are the same, for example: *je me lave* (I wash myself).

Forming reflexive verbs

French reflexive verbs follow patterns just like ordinary verbs, except that there is a pronoun between the subject and the verb. The pronouns are:

me	myself
te	yourself
se	himself, herself, itself
nous	ourselves
vous	yourself, yourselves
se	themselves

Note that French reflexive verbs are always accompanied by a pronoun, while in English the reflexive pronoun is optional.

Se laver (to wash oneself, to have a wash)

je me lave	I wash (myself)
tu te laves	you wash (yourself)
il/elle se lave	he/she/it washes (him-/her-/itself)
nous nous lavons	we wash (ourselves)
vous vous lavez	you wash (yourself/-selves)
ils/elles se lavent	they wash (themselves)

Useful reflexive verbs

s'amuser	to enjoy oneself
s'appeler*	to be called
s'asseoir*	to sit down
se battre*	to fight
se cacher	to hide
se coucher	to go to bed
se demander	to wonder
se dépêcher	to hurry
se déshabiller	to get undressed
se disputer	to argue
s'habiller	to get dressed
s'intéresser à	to be interested in
se laver	to wash oneself
se lever*	to get up
se rappeler*	to remember
se rencontrer	to meet
se reposer	to rest
se réveiller	to wake up
se sentir* mal	to feel sick
se taire*	to keep quiet
se tromper	to make a mistake
se trouver	to be found/situated

Giving orders

Reflexive verbs make their imperatives in the same way as ordinary verbs, but the pronoun comes after the verb, attached by a hyphen. To emphasize the *tu* form, *te* changes to *toi*:

e.g. *Lève-toi!*	Get up!
Levons-nous!	Let's get up!
Levez-vous!	Get up!

Fast facts

• The infinitive of reflexive verbs always begins with *se* (or *s′* if the verb starts with a vowel or an *h*).

• In English, we often omit the reflexive pronoun, and say things like "I'm hiding", rather than "I'm hiding myself".

Using negatives

To use a reflexive verb in the negative, you put *ne* between the subject and the pronoun, and *pas* after the verb.

Je ne me lève pas.
I'm not getting up.

Spot the difference

With reflexive verbs, the subject and object are the same:
e.g. *Il se lave.* (He washes himself.)

With ordinary verbs, the subject and object are different:
e.g. *Il lave la voiture.*
(He washes the car.)

Who and which

In French, you say *qui* and *que* for "who", "whom" and "which". Here are the rules for how to use them.

• *Qui* is used when the person or thing you're referring to is the subject of the sentence:
e.g. *l'homme* **qui** *est dans la maison* (the man **who** is in the house), or *le livre* **qui** *est dehors* (the book **which** is outside).

• *Que* is used when the person or thing you're referring to is the object of the verb:
e.g. *la femme* **que** *je connais* (the woman **whom** I know), or *le thé* **que** *tu bois* (the tea **which** you're drinking).

Telling the time

To answer *Quelle heure est-il?* (What time is it?) you say *Il est...* (It is...):

...midi/minuit

...une heure moins le quart

...huit heures moins dix

...dix heures et demie

...onze heures vingt

...trois heures

The Camembert treasure: chapter 10

Luc, Céline and Marion are at the school, looking for the next clue. They creep past the classrooms where different lessons are going on. Unknown to the three friends, they are still being followed...

New words

le crayon (de couleur)	crayon
le dessin	drawing
l'heure [f]	hour
l'indice [m]	clue
le ruban	ribbon
le signe	sign
le soir	evening
aimer	to like
couper	to cut
déchirer	to tear (up)
manquer	to be missing
revenir	to come back

Reflexive verbs:

se cacher	to hide
se calmer	to calm down
s'habiller	to get dressed
se lever	to get up
se réveiller	to wake up
se sentir* bien/mal	to feel well/ill
se trouver	to be found/ situated
à quelle heure	at what time, when
bien sûr	of course
huit heures	eight o'clock
neuf heures et quart	quarter past nine
parce que	because
pourquoi	why
sept heures et demie	half past seven
tout(e) seul(e)	all alone

Luc, Céline and Marion must wait for school to finish before they can sneak back to look at the old photograph.

Saying what you're doing

Faire is a common French verb which means "to do" or "to make". It has many different uses, including describing the weather (e.g. *il fait beau* - it's fine) and talking about an action (e.g. *faire du ski* - to go skiing).

Faire (to do, to make)

je fais	I do (am doing)
tu fais	you do
il/elle fait	he/she/it does
nous faisons	we do
vous faites	you do
ils/elles font	they do

Que fais-tu ce soir?
What are you doing this evening?

Expressions with *faire*

faire attention	to watch out
faire les courses	to go shopping
faire la cuisine	to cook
faire un film	to make a film
faire nuit	to be dark, to be night-time
faire des randonnées	to go hiking
faire du ski	to go skiing
faire de la voile	to go sailing

To get something done

Faire is also used to talk about having something done for you. You use *faire* + infinitive:
e.g. *Je fais réparer le toit.*
(I'm having the roof repaired.)

Talking about the weather

Often *il fait* is used with an adjective or a noun to describe the weather. To ask about the weather you say:
Quel temps fait-il?
(What's the weather like?)

Il fait beau.
It's fine.

Il fait chaud.
It's hot.

Il fait froid.
It's cold.

Il fait du vent.
It's windy.

In the middle of...

The present tense in French can be translated in two ways, so that *je fais* means both "I do" and "I am doing". To emphasize that you are in the middle of doing something, you can use the present tense of *être* + *en train de* + infinitive:

e.g. *Elle est en train de faire la cuisine.*
(She's in the middle of cooking.)

Saying because

Parce que means "because", so you
could say:
*Je veux un nouveau pull **parce que**
ce pull est vieux.* (I want a new
sweater **because** this sweater's old.)

To say "because of" you use *à
cause de*. For instance:
*Je reste ici **à cause de** la tempête.*
(I'm staying here **because of**
the storm.)

> *Je ne peux pas
> dormir à cause du bruit!*
> I can't sleep because
> of the noise!

Using *pour*

Pour has several uses. It can mean
"for", as in:
*C'est **pour** moi?* (Is it **for** me?)
Or it can be used with an infinitive to
mean "in order to", "so as to" or "to":

e.g. *Ils vont à la plage **pour** se
bronzer.* (They go to the beach **in
order to** sunbathe.)

You can also use *pour* as a simple
way of asking questions. Just add an
infinitive and say "please" at the end:

e.g. *Pour aller à la gare, s'il vous plaît?*
(How do I get to the station, please?)

> *Moi aussi!
> J'aime bien faire du
> ski dans les Alpes.*
> Me too! I like skiing in
> the Alpes.

> *Je suis contente
> à cause de la neige!*
> I'm happy because of
> the snow!

49

The Camembert treasure: chapter 11

Before Luc, Céline and Marion return to the school, the bald man tricks the principal with an impersonation and gets away with the photo...

Parce que c'est sa serviette.

New words

le gendarme	policeman
la gendarmerie	police station
le mécanicien	mechanic
la photocopieuse	photocopier
la pièce	part, room
la serviette	briefcase
emballer	to wrap (up)
emporter	to take (away)
entrer	to enter, to go in
fermer	to close, to shut
réparer	to repair, to mend
assez	quite, enough
bête	stupid, silly
ça, cela	that
cassé(e)	broken
demain matin	tomorrow morning

Bon, on emporte ça à la gendarmerie.

Outside the police station...

C'est fermé!

Bon, il faut revenir demain matin.

Est-ce que tu connais le gendarme?

Oui...il est assez sympa.

Pronouns

A pronoun is a short word that replaces the noun, such as "he" instead of "John" and "it" instead of "the car". *Je, tu, il, elle, nous, vous, ils* and *elles* are called **subject pronouns**, because they replace the subject of the sentence. **Object pronouns** are words like "him", "it" and "them", which replace the object of the sentence. In the sentence "I like them", "I" is the subject pronoun and "them" is the object pronoun.

Direct object pronouns

Object pronouns can either be direct or indirect. You use a direct object pronoun when you are replacing a noun which is the direct object of a sentence.

For instance, in the sentence *Pierre mange la glace*, you can replace *la glace* with **la**. The object pronoun always goes immediately before the verb, so *Pierre mange la glace* becomes *Pierre **la** mange*.

Pierre la mange. (Pierre is eating it.)

Here is a list of direct object pronouns:

me/m'[1]	me
te/t'[1]	you
le/l'[1]	him/it
la/l'[1]	her/it
nous	us
vous	you
les	them

With a negative, the pronoun still comes directly before the verb: e.g. *Elle ne **la** mange pas.* (She isn't eating **it**.)

[1] *m', t', l'* are used before a vowel.

Indirect object pronouns

If the object in a sentence can be preceded by the word "to", then it is known as indirect. So, in the sentence "I speak to Pierre", the indirect object is "Pierre". In French, the indirect object can be replaced by a different kind of pronoun, called an indirect object pronoun.

The indirect object pronouns are:

me/m'	(to) me
te/t'	(to) you
lui	(to) him/it
lui	(to) her/it
nous	(to) us
vous	(to) you
leur	(to) them

So the sentence *Je parle à Pierre* (I speak to Pierre) can be shortened to *Je **lui** parle* (I speak **to him**).

Emphatic pronouns

There is another set of pronouns, known as emphatic pronouns, which are slightly different from the ones above. They are: *moi* (me), *toi* (you), *lui* (him), *elle* (her), *nous* (us), *vous* (you), *eux* and *elles* (them).

Use them:
• after prepositions, e.g. *Ça appartient à **eux**.* (That belongs to **them**.)
• after *c'est*, e.g. *C'est **elle**.* (It's **her**.)
• on their own, e.g. *Qui est là? **Moi**!* (Who's there? **Me**!)

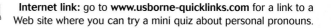
Word order

If you use two or more pronouns, there is a special order you must follow:

1	2	3
me	le/l'	lui
te	la/l'	leur
nous	les	
vous		

e.g. *Elle offre les bonbons à Malcolm.* (She offers the candy to Malcolm.)
OR
*Elle **les lui** offre.* (She offers **them to him**).

When there are two verbs in the sentence and the second one is in the infinitive, the object pronouns come between the verbs:
e.g. *On doit montrer la serviette à tes parents* (We should show the briefcase to your parents) becomes *On doit **la leur** montrer* (We should show **it to them**).
In the negative this becomes:
On ne doit pas la leur montrer. (We shouldn't show it to them.)

Passe-le moi!

When you use object pronouns with the imperative, you have to make a few changes first:

• *me* becomes *moi*
• *te* becomes *toi*
• the pronouns come after the verb and are joined by a hyphen:
e.g. *Donnez-moi le livre.*
(Give me the book.)
*Passe-**le** moi!* (Pass **it to me**!)

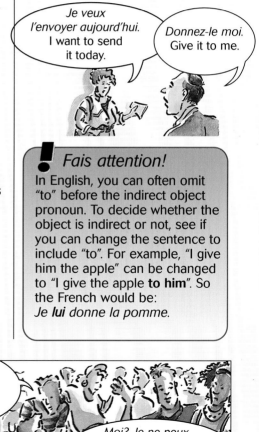

Je veux l'envoyer aujourd'hui. I want to send it today.

Donnez-le moi. Give it to me.

! Fais attention!

In English, you can often omit "to" before the indirect object pronoun. To decide whether the object is indirect or not, see if you can change the sentence to include "to". For example, "I give him the apple" can be changed to "I give the apple **to him**". So the French would be:
*Je **lui** donne la pomme.*

Tu aimes la musique africaine? Do you like African music?

Je veux danser avec toi. I want to dance with you.

Je l'adore! I love it!

Moi? Je ne peux pas danser comme eux! Me? I can't dance like them!

The Camembert treasure: chapter 12

Luc, Céline and Marion realize that in order to continue the hunt, they must first find the bald man. Perhaps his briefcase might be of some help...

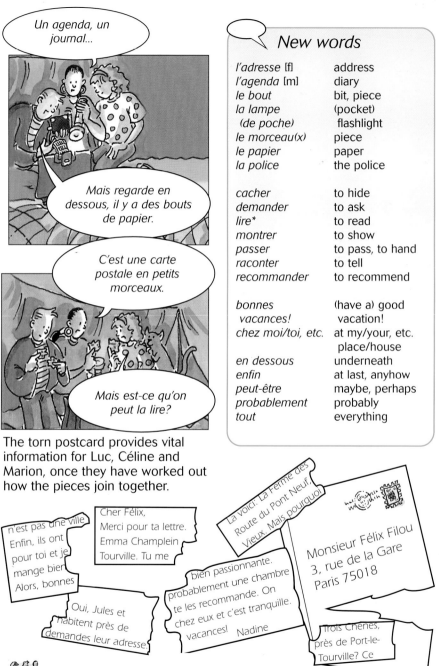

New words

l'adresse [f]	address
l'agenda [m]	diary
le bout	bit, piece
la lampe (de poche)	(pocket) flashlight
le morceau(x)	piece
le papier	paper
la police	the police
cacher	to hide
demander	to ask
lire*	to read
montrer	to show
passer	to pass, to hand
raconter	to tell
recommander	to recommend
bonnes vacances!	(have a) good vacation!
chez moi/toi, etc.	at my/your, etc. place/house
en dessous	underneath
enfin	at last, anyhow
peut-être	maybe, perhaps
probablement	probably
tout	everything

The torn postcard provides vital information for Luc, Céline and Marion, once they have worked out how the pieces join together.

Try writing out the postcard with all the pieces in the right order. Can you figure out what it says?

55

Using the imperfect tense

There are several tenses you can use to describe actions in the past. One of them is called the **imperfect**. In French, you use the imperfect to describe events that were in the process of happening or things that used to happened often, for example: *Hier j'étais en vacances* (Yesterday I was on vacation) or *Chaque samedi il regardait le foot* (Every Saturday he watched soccer).

Making the imperfect

To make the imperfect, you take the *nous* form of the present tense, remove the -*ons* and add a special set of endings to the stem. See how this works with the verb *finir*:

nous form of *finir* = *finissons*
minus -*ons* = *finiss*- (the stem)
plus -*ais*, -*ais*, -*ait*, -*ions*, -*iez*, -*aient*:

Finir (imperfect tense)

je finiss**ais**	I was finishing/ finished
tu finiss**ais**	you were finishing
il/elle finiss**ait**	he/she/it was finishing
nous finiss**ions**	we were finishing
vous finiss**iez**	you were finishing
ils/elles finiss**aient**	they were finishing

Que faisiez-vous hier soir à neuf heures?
What were you doing last night at nine o'clock?

Uh... Je me lavais les cheveux.
Umm... I was washing my hair.

Two useful imperfects

The two verbs that are used most frequently in the imperfect tense are *avoir* and *être*. The *nous* form of *être* (*nous sommes*) doesn't end in -*ons*, so to make the imperfect you use a different stem: *ét*-.

Avoir (imperfect tense)

j'av**ais**	I had/was having
tu av**ais**	you had
il/elle av**ait**	he/she/it had
nous av**ions**	we had
vous av**iez**	you had
ils/elles av**aient**	they had

Être (imperfect tense)

j'ét**ais**	I was/was being
tu ét**ais**	you were
il/elle ét**ait**	he/she/it was
nous ét**ions**	we were
vous ét**iez**	you were
ils/elles ét**aient**	they were

Fast facts

Être is the only verb that doesn't use the *nous* form minus -*ons* as its stem in the imperfect.
The imperfect stem for *être* is *ét*-.

Translating the imperfect

There are many different ways to translate the French imperfect tense into English:

• For actions that were in the process of happening, you can use "was" or "were" + a verb ending in "ing", e.g. *Je criais* (I **was** shout**ing**).

• For repeated or habitual actions in the past you often use "used to" or "would" + an infinitive, e.g. *Je jouais de la trompette chaque jour.* (I **used to** play the trumpet every day.)

• In English, you can often use the simple past tense ("I lived", "she went", etc.) to describe a repeated or continuous action in the past. This is sometimes known as the preterite, e.g. *Chaque été, Paul travaillait dans un café.* (Every summer, Paul work**ed** in a café.)

Using *y* and *en*

In French, the pronouns *y* and *en* are used in place of the prepositions *à* or *de* plus a noun.

• *y* is used to say "there". It replaces descriptions of places, such as *à la gare*: e.g. *J'étais à la gare* (I was at the station) becomes *J'y étais* (I was **there**).

• *y* is also used in the set phrase *il y a*, which means "there is" or "there are". In the imperfect, the phrase becomes *il y avait* (there was/were).

• *En* is used to say "some" or "any". It replaces *du, de la, de l'* or *des*, plus noun: e.g. *Je ne veux pas de fromage* (I don't want any cheese) becomes *Je n'en veux pas* (I don't want **any**).

• Sometimes you use *en* where in English you don't need a word at all: e.g. *Je veux un kilo de pommes* (I want a kilo of apples) becomes *J'en veux un kilo* (I want a kilo).

Henri regarde deux photos de lui quand il était petit.
(Henri is looking at two photos of himself when he was young.)

Il aimait jouer à la plage avec ses amis.
(He used to like playing on the beach with his friends.)

Chaque été il faisait du camping à la campagne.
(Each summer he would go camping in the country.)

The Camembert treasure: chapter 13

The next morning, they take the briefcase to the police, along with the photo of the bald man which Marion took at the harbor. But they don't get the response they were expecting...

After the trio have left the office...

New words

l'escroc [m]	crook, swindler
la famille	family
l'instituteur [m], l'institutrice [f]	teacher (in a junior school)
la poche	pocket
rapporter	to bring/take back
rentrer	to come/go (back/home)
voler	to steal, to rob
avant	before
ça suffit	that's enough
exactement	exactly
heureusement	fortunately
hier soir	yesterday evening
il y avait	there was/were
maintenant	now
probablement	probably
sans	without
tant pis	too bad
toujours	always
très	very
vite	quick(ly)

59

Using adverbs

Adverbs are words like "slowly" or "nicely" that give extra meaning to a verb. There are three main types:
- adverbs of **time** indicate **when** the action happens;
- adverbs of **place** describe **where** the action happens;
- adverbs of **manner** specify **how** the action happens.

How the action happens

French adverbs of manner are easy to spot because many are adjectives with -ment on the end (similar to the English "ly" ending):
e.g. *vrai + ment = vraiment*
(real + ly = really)

When the adjective ends with a consonant, the -ment ending is usually added to its feminine form, so *lent(e)* (slow) becomes *lentement* (slowly).

Je préfère aller plus lentement.
I prefer to go more slowly.

For longer adjectives ending in -ant or -ent, you remove the -nt and add -mment. So *intelligent* (intelligent) becomes *intelligemment* (intelligently).

A few exceptions

Some useful adverbs of manner which do not end in -ment are *bien* (well), *mal* (badly), *vite* (quickly) and *fort* (loudly).

Useful adverbs

Time

aujourd'hui	today
hier	yesterday
hier soir	yesterday evening, last night
avant-hier	the day before yesterday
demain	tomorrow
après-demain	the day after tomorrow
alors	then, so, well
déjà	already
d'habitude	usually, normally
parfois, de temps en temps	sometimes
souvent	often
toujours	always, still

Place

ici	here
là(-bas)	(over) there
loin (de)	far (from)
par ici	over/around here
partout	everywhere
près (de)	near (to)
quelque part	somewhere
nulle part	nowhere

Manner

beaucoup	a lot
exactement	exactly
heureusement	luckily, happily
lentement	slowly
peut-être	maybe
presque	almost, nearly
probablement	probably
vite	quickly
vraiment	really

Using two adverbs

In the sentence "the boy runs very quickly", "very" and "quickly" are both adverbs. "Very" describes how quickly the boy runs. This is called modifying the adverb.

Here is a list of French adverbs that can modify other adverbs or adjectives:

moins	less
plus	more
très	very
trop	too (as in "too much")

e.g. *Il marche trop vite!*
(He's walking too fast!)

Many years ago...

The phrase *il y a* means "there is" or "there are" (see page 57). However, it can also be used as an adverb of time, to mean "ago".

e.g. *Il y a quatre ans...*
(Four years **ago**...)

Word order

Some adverbs of time or place, such as *ici* and *souvent*, can either come at the beginning or the end of a phrase. For instance, you can either say *Ici on parle français* or *On parle français ici*. (We speak French here.)

In general, most adverbs go after the first verb in a phrase:
e.g. *Il pleut **trop** en Angleterre.*
(It rains too much in England.)

Il joue bien du saxo.
He plays the saxophone well.

Ses doigts bougent vite.
His fingers move quickly.

Il bat fort.
He hits hard.

Il joue souvent.
He plays often.

The Camembert treasure: chapter 14

After leaving the police station, Luc finds a note and an interesting magazine cutting in the bald man's diary. It seems that he has recently been involved in illegal activities...

Back at home, Marion shows Luc and Céline a very old letter written to her grandfather, Joseph. It's from the governor of the Wazorare islands. It tells how her great-grandfather, Clément, disappeared on one of the islands.

Wazorareville

Monsieur,

Malheureusement, votre père est très probablement mort. Il connaissait bien nos îles, mais lors de sa disparition il cherchait des plantes sur des îles dangereuses et très éloignées. Il était avec deux amis botanistes. Ils avaient un bon bateau, mais c'était la saison des tempêtes.

Pedro Paté
Gouverneur des îles

New words

l'an [m] l'année [f]	year
l'arrière-grand-père [m]	great-grandfather
le/la botaniste	botanist
la collection	collection
le couple	couple, pair
la disparition	disappearance
l'euro [m]	euro (currency)
le gouverneur	governor
l'habitant [m]	inhabitant
le perroquet	parrot
la plante	plant
la saison des tempêtes	stormy season
le salaire	pay, salary, fee
le temple	temple
attraper	to catch
avoir l'air	to look, to seem
bâtir	to build
étudier	to study
vénérer	to worship
voir*	to see
cent	a hundred
dangereux (dangereuse)	dangerous
dernier (dernière)	last
éloigné(e)	remote, faraway
intéressant(e)	interesting
il est interdit de	it is forbidden to
lors de	at the time of
malheureusement	unfortunately
mort(e)	dead
quelque chose	something

The perfect tense

The **perfect**, or *passé composé*, is the most common past tense used in French. It is used to talk about single actions that happened in the past and are now complete, for example: *Ma mère est allé à Paris.* (My mother went to Paris.)
In contrast, continuous or repeated past actions are described by the imperfect tense (see page 56).

How to form the perfect

The perfect tense is made up of two parts: the present tense of *avoir* or *être* (depending on which verb you are using), and a special form of the verb, called the **past participle** (p.p.):

e.g. *J'ai marché* (I walked)
present of *avoir* + p.p. of *marcher*

In these constructions, *avoir* and *être* are known as **auxiliary verbs** because they support the main verb. Most verbs make the perfect tense with *avoir*. To find out which verbs use *être*, go to page 68.

Regular past participles

For regular verbs, it is easy to form the past participle.

• With ER verbs you remove the *-er* and add **é**, e.g. *trouver - trouvé*.

• With IR verbs you just remove the *-r*, e.g. *choisir - choisi*.

• With RE verbs you remove the *-re* and add **u**, e.g. *perdre - perdu*.

J'ai trouvé mes clés!
(I've found my keys!)

> *Qu'as-tu fait hier soir?*
> What did you do yesterday evening?

> *J'ai fini mon livre et j'ai regardé la télé.*
> I finished my book and I watched TV.

Irregular past participles

For irregular verbs you have to learn the past participles separately. Here are some useful irregular participles. They all use the auxiliary verb *avoir*.

avoir - eu	(had)
boire - bu	(drunk)
connaître - connu	(known)
devoir - dû	(had to)
être - été	(been)
faire - fait	(made, done)
lire - lu	(read)
mettre - mis	(put)
prendre - pris	(taken)
pouvoir - pu	(been able to)
savoir - su	(known)
voir - vu	(seen)
vouloir - voulu	(wanted)

The expression *il faut* (it is necessary) is irregular, and in the perfect it becomes *il a fallu* (it was necessary).

Agreement of the participle

When a direct object comes before a verb in the perfect tense, the participle must agree with it, just like an adjective:

• For feminine direct objects, add **e** to the past participle:
e.g. *La tour? Je l'ai vue.*
(The tower? I've seen it.)

• For masculine or mixed plurals, add **s**:
e.g. *Les biscuits? Il les a mangés.*
(The biscuits? He ate them.)

• For feminine plurals, add **es**:
e.g. *Les clés? Nous les avons trouvées.*
(The keys? We've found them.)

Perfect or imperfect?

Often you will find both the imperfect and the perfect tense in one sentence. The imperfect tense is used to set the scene, describe how things were, and talk about continuous actions. The perfect tense is used for actions which interrupt or alter the situation:

e.g. *Je lisais un livre quand le téléphone a sonné.*
(I was reading a book when the phone rang.)

Fast facts

• If you're describing a one-off event that is over and done with, use the perfect tense.

• If you're setting the scene in the past, or talking of something that was in the process of happening, use the imperfect tense.

Tu as une nouvelle moto?
Have you got a new motorcycle?

Je l'ai vue hier. Elle est superbe!
I saw it yesterday. It's gorgeous!

Merci. Je l'ai achetée au weekend.
Thanks. I bought it on the weekend.

65

The Camembert treasure: chapter 15

While they're waiting for lunch, the three friends read in the bald man's diary how he came across details of the Camembert treasure...

New words

le coffre	chest (container)
le déjeuner	lunch
l'entrée [f]	entrance
la grotte	cave
le pain	bread
le perroquet	parrot
la réunion	meeting
*atteindre**	to reach, to get to
*attendre**	to wait
expliquer	to explain
*mettre**	to put
oublier	to forget
parler	to speak
réussir (à)	to succeed (in)
*voir**	to see
à table	come and sit down
bientôt	soon
ça ne fait rien	it doesn't matter
comment	how
dedans	inside
il va arriver	he's going to arrive
long(ue)	long
Papa	Dad, Daddy
pardon	sorry
presque	almost
prêt(e)	ready
rouillé(e)	rusty

The perfect tense with *être*

The perfect tense of a small group of verbs is formed with the present tense of *être*, not *avoir*, for example: *Je suis allé* (I went). Verbs which take *être* in the perfect tense include all reflexive verbs (see page 44) and a group of 13 common verbs.

Verbs with *être*

The group of verbs taking *être* all seem to refer either to a **change of place** or a **change of state** (going, coming, dying, etc.). If a verb takes *être,* it is likely that its opposite does as well: e.g. *mourir* and *naître.*

Here is a list of the 13 main verbs which take *être.* The irregular past participles are shown in brackets.

*aller**	to go
arriver	to arrive
*descendre**	to go down(stairs)
entrer	to enter
monter	to go up(stairs)
*mourir** (mort)*	to die
*naître** (né)*	to be born
*partir**	to leave
rester	to stay
retourner	to go back
*sortir**	to go out
tomber	to fall (over)
*venir** (venu)*	to come

Agreement

For verbs taking *être*, the past participle almost always agrees with the subject (see the *Fais attention!* box for exception to the rule):

e.g. *Les femmes sont arrivées.* (The women have arrived.)

Reflexive verbs

To make the perfect tense of a reflexive verb, such as *se laver*, you put the present tense of *être* between the reflexive pronoun and the past participle of the verb. Remember to make the necessary agreements:

je me suis lavé(e)
tu t'es lavé(e)
il s'est lavé
elle s'est lavée
nous nous sommes lavé(e)s
vous vous êtes lavé(e)s
ils se sont lavés
elles se sont lavées

Je suis arrivé ce matin.
I arrived this morning.

! *Fais attention!*

Reflexive verbs don't agree with the subject when there is a direct object following the verb:

e.g. *Elle s'est lavé les mains.* (She washed her hands.)

Making the negative

To make the negative of a verb in the perfect tense, put *ne* and *pas* on either side of the auxiliary verb: e.g. *Elle n'est pas rentrée hier soir.* (She didn't go home last night.) For reflexive verbs, the pronoun goes after the *ne*, for instance: *Je ne me suis pas reposé.* (I haven't rested.)

Fast facts

Verbs ending with *-venir* and *-entrer* also take *être* in the perfect tense.

The main ones are:
• *devenir (devenu)* - to become
• *revenir (revenu)* - to come back
• *rentrer* - to go back home

Making questions

You can ask questions in any tense. Sometimes when you ask a question in the perfect tense, the word order changes. Here are the different ways to ask a question, using the example: "Has he arrived?"

• Just add a question mark: *Il est arrivé?*

• Add *est-ce que:* **Est-ce qu'**il est arrivé?

• Make an inversion: **Est-il** arrivé?

To stop the sentence from sounding awkward, you sometimes add a *t* between *a* and *il* or *elle*:

e.g. *A-t-elle trouvé les clés?* (Has she found the keys?)

Guillaume s'est levé tard ce matin.
Guillaume woke up late this morning.

Il s'est habillé vite et il s'est dépêché d'aller à l'école...
He dressed quickly and hurried to school...

...mais il était quand même en retard.
...but he was still late.

Et malheureusement, c'est lui le prof!
And unfortunately, he's the teacher!

69

The Camembert treasure: chapter 16

After lunch, Luc, Céline and Marion go to the farm where the crook, Félix Filou, is staying. When they arrive, they overhear a conversation that will take them to the next clue...

New words

le jardin public	park
la pierre	stone
la ruine	ruin
retrouver	to find (again)
au bord de	by (the side of)
beau (belle)	beautiful, good-looking
en ruine	ruined, in ruins
prochain(e)	next
quelques	a few
seulement	only

Using the perfect and possessives

The French perfect tense is used for two different tenses in English: the perfect and the simple past. For example, *il a volé* can be translated as "he has stolen" (perfect tense) and "he stole" (simple past). Both *volé* and "stolen" are past participles and can be used as adjectives to describe a noun.

Making adjectives

The French past participle can be used as an adjective, coming after the noun and agreeing with it:

e.g. *des objets* **volés**
(stolen goods)
e.g. *des indices* **cachés**
(hidden clues)

Several actions

When the subject of a sentence does more than one action in the perfect tense, it is not necessary to repeat the auxiliary verb. So "I ate ice-cream and drank lemonade" becomes *J'ai mangé de la glace et bu de la limonade.*

Hier soir... (Yesterday evening...)

j'ai téléphoné à ma sœur...
I phoned my sister...

écrit une lettre...
wrote a letter...

et mangé mon dîner.
and ate my dinner.

Fast facts

• The French perfect tense is called a compound tense because it has two parts to it. The first part is the present tense of the auxiliary verb (*avoir* or *être*) and the second part is the past participle (p.p.):

e.g. *Les enfants sont partis.*
subject + auxiliary verb + p.p.
(The children have left.)

This one, that one

To distinguish between objects or people in French, you use a special pronoun *celui*, plus *-ci* (here) or *-là* (there):

[m]	[f]	
celui-ci	celle-ci	this one
celui-là	celle-là	that one
ceux-ci	celles-ci	these
ceux-là	celles-là	those

e.g. *Ces crayons sont à qui?*
Celui-ci *est à moi et* **ceux-là** *sont à Paul.*
(Whose are the crayons?
This one's mine and **those** are Paul's.)

Mine, yours, his, etc.

In French, there are two ways to say "mine, "yours" and so on.

To say something like "the ball is mine", you use the preposition *à* followed by a pronoun: *le ballon est à moi*. This list shows which pronouns you should use:

à moi	mine
à toi	yours
à lui	his
à elle	hers
à nous	ours
à vous	yours
à eux/elles	theirs

To say something like "mine is green", you use a different set of words. These are called **possessive pronouns** and they change to agree with the noun they are replacing. So, talking about *une porte* (a door), you could say: *La mienne est blanche*. (Mine is white.)

Possessive pronouns

Singular

[m]	[f]	
le mien	*la mienne*	mine
le tien	*la tienne*	yours
le sien	*la sienne*	hers/his/its
le nôtre	*la nôtre*	ours
le vôtre	*la vôtre*	yours
le leur	*la leur*	theirs

Plural

[m]	[f]	
les miens	*les miennes*	mine
les tiens	*les tiennes*	yours
les siens	*les siennes*	hers/his/its
les nôtre	*les nôtres*	ours
les vôtres	*les vôtres*	yours
les leurs	*les leurs*	theirs

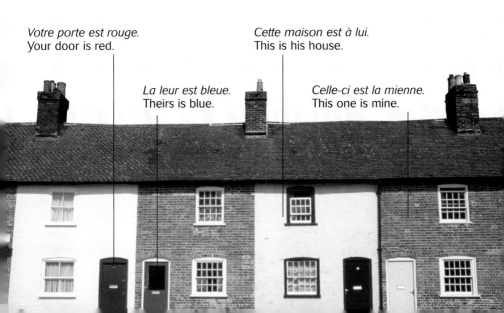

Votre porte est rouge.
Your door is red.

Cette maison est à lui.
This is his house.

La leur est bleue.
Theirs is blue.

Celle-ci est la mienne.
This one is mine.

The Camembert treasure: chapter 17

Luc, Céline and Marion go home to get their bikes and rush to the ruined tower to find the next clue before Félix gets there. It takes them quite a while to find it...

Soon they are at the tower ruins.

Rien! J'ai regardé partout et examiné chaque pierre.

Eh, j'ai trouvé quelque chose ici!

Regardez!... C'est le signe de Clément Camembert!

The three friends have found Clément Camembert's sign on an old plaque.

Nous avons gardé cette tour en ruine, parce que c'est un monument sacré pour les habitants de Tourville.

Les pirates de l'île des Pirates l'ont détruite il y a trois ans, mais maintenant nous nous sommes vengés. Nous avons gagné notre dernière bataille contre eux, nous les avons chassés de leur fort sur l'île et ils ont disparu de notre pays.

New words

la bataille	battle
la clôture	fence
le fort	fort
l'habitant [m]	inhabitant
le monument	monument
le pays	country
le pirate	pirate
avoir* besoin de	to need
chasser	to chase (away)
déchiffrer	to decipher
détruire* (p.p. *détruit*)	to destroy
disparaître* (p.p. *disparu*)	to disappear
examiner	to examine
explorer	to explore
gagner	to win
garder	to keep
se venger	to get revenge
chaque	each
dernier, dernière	last
donc	so, therefore
ne...pas encore	not yet
sacré(e)	sacred
tout de suite	right away

The words of the plaque give them a good idea of where they must go next. Translate it and see what you think...

The future tense

In French there are several ways of expressing the future:
- you can use the future tense (see below);
- you can use the verb *aller* (to go) with an infinitive, just as we do in English, e.g. *je vais donner* (I'm going to give);
- you can simply indicate the future by using a word like *demain* (tomorrow) with the present tense.

Making the future tense

The future endings are:
-ai, -as, -a, -ons, -ez, -ont.
With most ER and IR verbs you just take the infinitive and add these endings. Here you can see how with the verb *donner* (to give):

Donner (future)

je donnerai	I will give
tu donneras	you will give
il/elle donnera	he/she/it will give
nous donnerons	we will give
vous donnerez	you will give
ils/elles donneront	they will give

Je te donnerai ton cadeau ce soir, Papa.
I'll give you your present this evening, Dad.

Verbs ending in *-re*

For most verbs ending in *-re*, you remove the final *-e* of the infinitive before adding the future endings. For example, the future stem of *prendre* is *prendr-*.

Irregular future stems

There are some verbs that do not use the infinitive to form the future tense. Instead they have their own future stem. Here are some common irregular future stems:

aller (to go) - *ir*
avoir (to have) - *aur*
courir (to run) - *courr*
devoir (to have to) - *devr*
envoyer (to send) - *enverr*
être (to be) - *ser*
faire (to make, to do) - *fer*
falloir (to be necessary) - *faudr*
mourir (to die) - *mourr*
pleuvoir (to rain) - *pleuvr*
pouvoir (to be able to) - *pourr*
recevoir (to receive) - *recevr*
savoir (to know) - *saur*
venir (to come) - *viendr*
voir (to see) - *verr*
vouloir (to want) - *voudr*

All verbs ending in *-oir* have an irregular future stem.

Learning tip

The first three endings of the future tense are easy to remember because they are the same as the verb *avoir* in the present tense (*ai, as, a*).

Using the present

Sometimes both French and English use the present tense when talking about future events:
e.g. *Il vient ce soir.*
(He's coming this evening.)
The time words ("tomorrow", "this evening", etc.) indicate that the action will happen in the future, so you don't need to use the future tense.

Je pars demain matin!
I'm leaving tomorrow morning!

Quand + future tense

In French sentences with *quand* (when), you use the future tense, where in English you would use the present. For instance, in English you say: "When Paul arrives (present), we'll leave (future)". In French you would say: *Quand Paul arrivera* (future), *nous partirons* (future).

Going to...

In both French and English, you can also express the future by using the verb "to go", e.g. *je vais ouvrir la porte.* (I'm going to open the door.) This is fairly common in French, especially when talking about events that are just about to happen. You take the present tense of *aller* (to go) and add an infinitive. So, "I'm going to make a cake" would be *Je vais faire un gâteau.*

Fast facts

The three ways of talking about future events are:

• infinitive or future stem + *-ai, -as, -a, -ons, -ez, -ont*

• *aller* (present tense) + infinitive

• present tense of verb + time word indicating the future

Quand Michel arrivera en Amérique, il fera des randonnées.
When Michel arrives in America, he'll go hiking.

The Camembert treasure: chapter 18

Luc, Céline and Marion need to go to the fort on Pirates' Island, but it's too late to go that night. Just in case Félix finds the clue and gets ahead of them, they devise a very crafty way of throwing him off the scent...

New words

le barreau(x)	(window) bar
le bijou(x)	jewel
le bois	wood
la direction	direction
l'endroit [m]	place
la feuille	leaf
la fortune	fortune
le mur	wall
la nuit	night
le panneau(x)	panel
le piège	trap
la piste	trail
la tâche	task
déranger	to disturb
dessiner	to draw
laisser	to leave
tomber dans le piège	to fall in the trap
à l'intérieur	inside
certainement	certainly, definitely
faux (fausse)	false
génial(e)	wonderful
mauvais(e)	wrong, bad
par là	over there
pendant	during

Marion writes a note to confuse the crook and put him on a false trail.

C.C. ueidA. àl tnores enutrof am te χuojib sem suoT. siob ne χuaennap sed ceva rum nu sarevuort ut, rueirétni'l À. àl rap sarertne uT. χuaerrab snas ertênef enu sarrev uT. χueiV-el-troP eđ eiremradneg al à rella arduaf lI. eliciffid ares ellE. ehcât erèinred at icioV. séssial ia'j euq secidni sel suot évuort sa ut. tnanetniaM, slif noM

Can you read Marion's writing and find out where she is sending Félix the crook?

The Camembert treasure: chapter 19

That evening, the policeman who didn't believe the three friends' story stumbles across Félix Filou's picture in the wanted files. Then he lands a catch he hadn't been anticipating...

Meanwhile, outside the police station...

New words

le détail	detail
l'enfant [m]	child
le numéro	number
la vitre	window pane
le vol	theft
aider	to help
arrêter	to stop, to arrest
casser	to break
faxer	to fax
ouvrir*	to open
enfin	at last
peut-être	perhaps
recherché(e)	sought after, wanted
41 ans	41 years old

Making comparisons

Most comparisons in French are made by using *plus* (more) or *le/la/les plus* (the most) before an adjective or an adverb, for example: *l'homme le plus rapide* (the fastest man) or *marche plus lentement* (walk more slowly). To say "less" or "the least", you use *moins* in the same way as *plus*, for example: *il est moins fatigué* (he's less tired).

Comparisons with adjectives

The French for "Annie is **smaller**" is *Annie est plus petite*. *Petit* has an **e** on the end to agree with the feminine noun *Annie*. To say "Annie is **the smallest**", you add *la*: *Annie est la plus petite*.

le plus grand
the biggest

la plus petite
the smallest

plus grand
bigger

Before or after the noun

Unlike most other adjectives, *grand* and *petit* belong to a group of adjectives that come before the noun (see page 12). But when you are making comparisons, they can come before or after:
e.g. *Annie est la plus petite fille* or *Annie est la fille la plus petite*.

In most cases, *plus* + adjective come after the noun:
e.g. *Le pays le plus chaud*.
(The hottest country.)
Les garçons les plus intelligents.
(The most intelligent boys.)

Less, the least

To make comparisons such as "less interesting" and "the least difficult" you use *moins* (less) in the same way as *plus*, and *le moins* (the least) in the same way as *le plus*:
e.g. *Cette matière est moins intéressante*.
(This subject is less interesting.)
Le sport le moins difficile.
(The least difficult sport.)

Comparisons with adverbs

With adverbs you also use *plus* and *le plus*, but there is no agreement because they are describing the action, not the noun:
e.g. *Il marche plus lentement*.
(He walks more slowly.)
Elle parle le plus couramment.
(She speaks the most fluently.)

Fast facts

• *Moins/le moins* means "less/the least" and can be used in the same way as *plus/le plus*.

• Adverbs never change to make agreements. Likewise, when used with an adverb, *le plus* never changes to *la* or *les plus*.

Some exceptions

A few French adjectives and adverbs do not use *plus* and *le plus* to make comparisons. Instead, they have irregular forms:

Adjectives

bon(ne)	*meilleur(e)*	*le/la/les meilleur(e)(s)*
good	better	the best
mauvais(e)	*pire*	*le/la/les pire(s)*
bad	worse	the worst

Adverbs

bien	*mieux*	*le mieux*
well	better	the best
mal	*pire*	*le pire*
badly	worse	the worst
beaucoup	*plus*	*le plus*
much	more	the most
peu	*moins*	*le moins*
little	less	the least

Bigger than, smaller than

In English, we link the two things we are comparing with "than" (e.g. Peter is bigger than Paul, the violin is smaller than the cello, etc.). In French, the linking word is *que*:
e.g. *Il est plus grand **que** sa sœur.*
(He's taller **than** his sister.)
*Les serpents sont plus dangereux **que** les escargots.*
(Snakes are more dangerous **than** snails.)

As...as

To compare things that are similar, English uses "as...as" and French uses *aussi...que*:
e.g. *Son ami est **aussi** bête **que** lui.*
(His friend is **as** stupid **as** he is.)
*Mon allemand est **aussi** mauvais **que** mon français.*
(My German is **as** bad **as** my French.)

Les voiles les plus hautes sont aussi celles les plus petites.
The highest sails are also the smallest ones.

Ce bateau est beaucoup plus grand que les autres.
This boat is much bigger than the others.

Ce bateau est plus près.
This boat is nearer.

Celui-là est plus loin.
That one is further away.

The Camembert treasure: chapter 20

The next morning, the three friends borrow Jérôme's boat to cross to Pirates' Island. They get inside the ruined fort, but can they find the treasure and get out again?

The three friends must go to the end of the longest tunnel. They measure the tunnels using footsteps. Luc and Marion each take one and Céline does the other two.

New words

le cachot	dungeon
le fort	fort
la grille	gate
la rame	oar
la serviette	towel
le souterrain	underground passage, tunnel
emprunter	to borrow
prêter	to lend
ramer	to row
tourner en rond	to go around in circles
au bout de	at/to the end of
au secours!	help!
autre	other, another
bizarre	weird, strange
court(e)	short
encore	even, again, more
mouillé(e)	wet
plein(e) de	full of, lots of

Do you know which tunnel they must take?

85

Conditional sentences

A conditional action is one that depends on something else happening. In both French and English you often use a special form of the verb, called the **conditional**, to describe conditional actions, for example: *Je marcherais, mais il fait trop chaud.* (I would walk, but it's too hot.) The conditional is also used in polite expressions, for example: *Voudriez-vous du thé?* (Would you like some tea?)

Making the conditional

If you know the future tense and the imperfect tense, the conditional is very easy. You take the stem of the future tense (which is usually the infinitive of the verb) and add the imperfect endings:
(*-ais, -ais, -ait, -ions, -iez, -aient*).

Marcher (conditional)

je marcher**ais**	I would walk
tu marcher**ais**	you would walk
il/elle marcher**ait**	he/she/it would walk
nous marcher**ions**	we would walk
vous marcher**iez**	you would walk
ils/elles marcher**aient**	they would walk

J'achetèrais cette maison, mais je n'ai pas d'argent.
I would buy this house, but I don't have any money.

If...

There are some conditional actions that are not expressed using the conditional tense. In sentences using "if", or *si* in French, you sometimes use the present or future tense to describe a conditional action.

There are normally two parts to a *si* sentence:
e.g. *Si tu réussis* (**si clause**), *on organisera une fête* (**consequence**). (If you succeed, we'll have a party.)

When the *si* clause is in the present tense, you use the same tenses for the consequence in French as you would do in English:
e.g. *Si j'ai le temps, je viendrai.* (If I have time, I'll come.)
Si le prof sort, les enfants jouent. (If the teacher goes out, the children play.)

You can also switch out the *si* clause and the consequence and say:
Les enfants jouent si le prof sort. (The children play if the teacher goes out.)

Fast facts

Si clause	Consequence
Si + present tense	present or future tense

86

Less likely events

You also use "if" clauses to talk about events that are less likely to happen. This could be something you dream about, such as winning the lottery or releasing a hit record. In French, the tenses used for less likely events are:

Si + imperfect, then conditional
e.g. *Si je gagnais la loterie, j'achèterais un yacht.* (If I won the lottery, I would buy a yacht.)

Si j'étais reine, je mangerais bien chaque jour.
If I were queen, I would eat well every day.

Fast facts

Si clause	Consequence
Si + imperfect tense	conditional tense

Polite conversation

The conditional is often used in polite conversation. The most polite way to ask a question is to use the *vous* form of the conditional:
e.g. *Aimeriez-vous m'aider?* (Would you like to help me?)
e.g. *Pourriez-vous me prêter dix francs?* (Would you be able to lend me ten francs?)

S'il te/vous plaît

S'il te plaît and *s'il vous plaît* both mean "please". Word for word, the whole expression translates as "if it to you is pleasing". The first word is in fact *si* (if) which shortens to *s'* before a vowel.

Qu'est-ce que vous feriez si vous trouviez un trésor?
(What would you do if you found some treasure?)

Je ferais une croisière.
I would go on a cruise.

J'irais à la lune.
I would go to the moon.

87

The Camembert treasure: chapter 21

The three friends select the longest tunnel. Now, if there's any treasure to be found, surely they must be close...

Meanwhile, the policeman has gone to the Camembert house...

Bonjour, je voudrais parler à Marion, Luc et Céline.

Je voudrais les remercier. Ils m'ont aidé à attraper un escroc!

Aimeriez-vous les attendre?

Non, je reviendrai. Je ne voudrais pas vous déranger.

Mais d'abord vous pourriez peut-être nous raconter l'histoire. Nous n'en savons rien!

New words

l'anneau(x) [m]	ring
le fer	iron
l'histoire [f]	history, story
la lampe	lamp
le mur	wall
aider	to help
attraper	to catch
déranger	to disturb
remercier	to thank
revenir*	to come back
se terminer	to end
assez de	enough
d'abord	first
dessus	on top of (it)
ici	here
mieux	better
peut-être	perhaps
si	if

Writing a letter in French

There are two main types of letters: informal (for friends and family) and formal (for companies and people you don't know). Here are some basic guidelines for writing letters in French.

Structure

Every letter has a basic structure. Normally, you put your town or full address in the top right-hand corner, followed by the date. At the end, you sign off with an appropriate farewell.

The date

If the date is Tuesday 7th September, you can either write *mardi 7 septembre* or simply *le 7 septembre*. The initial letter of the day or the month is lower-case and the number doesn't need anything after it, unless it is the first day of the month when you write *1er* (short for *premier*).

Paris, le 25 octobre

Chère Suzanne,

Je te remercie de ta lettre. Ça va chez toi? Je suis très contente parce que j'ai gagné deux billets pour un concert à Bercy. Viens avec moi! On passera une soirée fantastique et tu peux rester chez moi.

Écris-moi vite ta réponse.

Grosses bises,

Julie

Informal letters

The French for "dear" is *cher*. You use it when writing to friends and family and people you know very well. Because *cher* is an adjective, you have to make it agree with the noun which follows.
• Before a male name you write *cher*, e.g. *Cher Luc*.
• Before a female name you write *chère*, e.g. *Chère Marion*.
• Before more than one male name or a mixture of male and female names you use *chers*, e.g. *Chers Luc et Céline*.
• Before more than one female name you use *chères*, e.g. *Chères Marion et Céline*.

Useful phrases

• *Je te remercie de...* (Thanks for...) e.g. *Je te remercie de ta lettre.* (Thanks for your letter.)
• *J'ai été très content(e) d'avoir de tes nouvelles.* (It was lovely to hear from you.)
• *Dis bonjour à...* (Say hello to...) e.g. *Dis bonjour à ta mère pour moi.* (Say hello to your Mom for me.)
• *Écris-moi.* (Write to me.)

Signing off

Use *Amitiés* (regards, best wishes) for people you know quite well and *Gros baisers* or *Grosses bises* (the equivalent of "love from" or "love and kisses") for close friends and family.

Signing off

The usual way to finish a letter to a firm or someone you don't know is: *Je vous prie d'agréer, Monsieur* (or *Madame* or *Messieurs*), *l'assurance de mes sentiments distingués.* The equivalent in English is "Yours faithfully".

Formal letters

If you're writing to someone, or a group of people, that you've never met before, you leave out *cher* and just write:
• *Messieurs* (Sirs) to a company
• *Monsieur* (Sir) to a man
• *Madame* (Madam) to a woman
If the person is important and you know their position, you can include it. For example, you would write *Monsieur/Madame le Maire* to the mayor and *Monsieur/Madame le Ministre* to a government minister.

Useful phrases

• *Je vous prie de...* (Please...)
• *Je vous serais reconnaissant(e) de...* (I would be grateful if you would...)
• *Suite à...* (Further to...)
e.g. *Suite à notre conversation téléphonique...* (Further to our telephone conversation...)
• *Je désirerais/Je voudrais...* (I wish to/I would like to...)
e.g. *Je désirerais réserver une chambre.*
(I wish to reserve a room.)
• *Veuillez confirmer...*
(Please confirm...)
• *Veuillez trouver ci-joint...*
(Please find enclosed...)

59 Kipling Street
London SE1 3RZ

le 29 juillet

Monsieur,

Cet été, je vais en vacances avec ma famille et je désirerais en savoir plus sur la vallée de la Loire. Je vous serais reconnaissant de m'envoyer des renseignements sur cette région et surtout sur les terrains de camping.

Je vous prie d'agréer, Monsieur, l'assurance de mes sentiments distingués,

Paul Smith

How do I make the conditional of the verb *désirer*?

The Camembert treasure: chapter 22

Back at the old fort, they've found the treasure, and now just have to find a way out since the entrance has been jammed by fallen rocks...

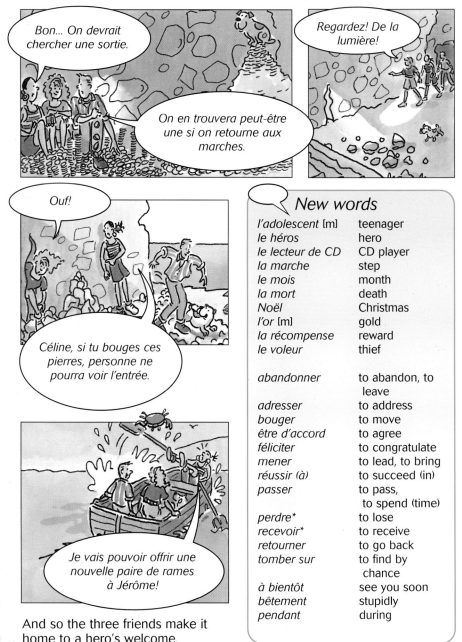

Bon... On devrait chercher une sortie.

On en trouvera peut-être une si on retourne aux marches.

Regardez! De la lumière!

Ouf!

Céline, si tu bouges ces pierres, personne ne pourra voir l'entrée.

Je vais pouvoir offrir une nouvelle paire de rames à Jérôme!

New words

l'adolescent [m]	teenager
le héros	hero
le lecteur de CD	CD player
la marche	step
le mois	month
la mort	death
Noël	Christmas
l'or [m]	gold
la récompense	reward
le voleur	thief
abandonner	to abandon, to leave
adresser	to address
bouger	to move
être d'accord	to agree
féliciter	to congratulate
mener	to lead, to bring
réussir (à)	to succeed (in)
passer	to pass, to spend (time)
perdre*	to lose
recevoir*	to receive
retourner	to go back
tomber sur	to find by chance
à bientôt	see you soon
bêtement	stupidly
pendant	during

And so the three friends make it home to a hero's welcome.

Once Luc and Céline are back home in Paris, Marion sends them a letter and a cutting from the local newspaper...

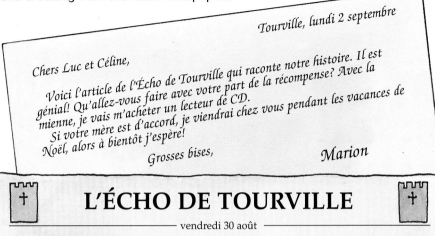

Tourville, lundi 2 septembre

Chers Luc et Céline,

Voici l'article de l'Écho de Tourville qui raconte notre histoire. Il est génial! Qu'allez-vous faire avec votre part de la récompense? Avec la mienne, je vais m'acheter un lecteur de CD.
Si votre mère est d'accord, je viendrai chez vous pendant les vacances de Noël, alors à bientôt j'espère!

Grosses bises,

Marion

L'ÉCHO DE TOURVILLE

— vendredi 30 août —

Le trésor de la famille Camembert

Marion Camembert avec ses amis, Luc et Céline Meunier, et son chien, Toudou.

Félix Filou, le voleur d'oiseaux rares qui voulait voler le trésor de la famille Camembert.

Pour Marion Camembert et ses amis Luc et Céline, cela a été un mois d'août passionnant. Ils ont aidé la police à attraper un escroc, Félix Filou.

Il y a quelques mois, Filou était sur une des îles Wazorare. Il y cherchait des perroquets très rares qu'il voulait voler. Il est tombé sur une lettre de Clément, l'arrière-grand-père de Marion. C'était une vieille lettre adressée à Joseph, le grand-père de Marion, et abandonnée sur l'île dans un vieux coffre après la mort de Clément. La lettre était le premier indice dans une chasse au trésor. Elle a mené Filou à Tourville où, bêtement, il l'a perdue. Luc et Céline, qui venaient passer quelques jours avec leur amie Marion, l'ont trouvée. Les trois adolescents ont réussi à trouver le trésor (de l'or), caché dans le vieux Fort des Pirates, avant l'escroc, et ils ont aidé la police à l'attraper.

Les trois héros ont aussi reçu une récompense de 2 000 euros de la police. Nous les félicitons!

Numbers and other useful words

Les nombres [f] (numbers)

0	zéro	18	dix-huit
1	un	19	dix-neuf
2	deux	20	vingt
3	trois	21	vingt et un
4	quatre	22	vingt-deux
5	cinq	23	vingt-trois
6	six	30	trente
7	sept	31	trente et un
8	huit	40	quarante
9	neuf	50	cinquante
10	dix	60	soixante
11	onze	70	soixante-dix
12	douze	71	soixante et onze
13	treize	72	soixante-douze
14	quatorze	80	quatre-vingts
15	quinze	81	quatre-vingt-un
16	seize	90	quatre-vingt-dix
17	dix-sept	91	quatre-vingt-onze

100	cent
101	cent un
150	cent cinquante
200	deux cents
201	deux cent un
300	trois cents

1,000[1]	mille
1,100	mille cent
1,200	mille deux cent
2,000	deux mille
2,100	deux mille cent
10,000	dix mille
100,000	cent mille
1,000,000[1]	un million

1st	1er/1ère	(le) premier, (la) première
2nd	2ème	(le/la) deuxième
3rd	3ème	(le/la) troisième
9th	9ème	(le/la) neuvième

[1]In French, you leave a space instead of using a comma and write 1 000, 1 000 000, etc.

Les jours [m] (days)

lundi [m]	Monday
mardi [m]	Tuesday
mercredi [m]	Wednesday
jeudi [m]	Thursday
vendredi [m]	Friday
samedi [m]	Saturday
dimanche [m]	Sunday

Les mois [m] (months)

janvier	January
février	February
mars	March
avril	April
mai	May
juin	June
juillet	July
août	August
septembre	September
octobre	October
novembre	November
décembre	December

Les dates [f] (dates)

Quelle est la date?	What's the date?
lundi	on Monday
le lundi	on Mondays
en août, au mois d'août	in August
le premier avril	April the first
le trois janvier	January the third
mardi 7 mars	Tuesday March 7

Les années [m] (years)

1980	mille neuf cent quatre-vingts
2000	l'an deux mille
2001	deux mille un
2002	deux mille deux
2010	deux mille dix

Les saisons [f] (seasons)

le printemps	spring
l'été [m]	summer
l'automne [m]	autumn
l'hiver [m]	winter

Le temps (weather)

le climat	climate
la météo	weather forecast
la température	temperature
Quel temps fait-il?	What's the weather like?
Il fait beau	It's fine
Il fait chaud	It's hot
Il fait du soleil	It's sunny
Il fait froid	It's cold
Il fait mauvais	It's bad
Il neige	It's snowing
Il pleut	It's raining
Il y a du brouillard	It's foggy
Il y a du verglas	It's icy
Le soleil brille	The sun's shining
la foudre	lightning
le gel	frost
la grêle	hail
le neige	snow
le nuage	cloud
l'orage [m]	storm
la pluie	rain
le soleil	sun
le tonnerre	thunder

Useful words

à bientôt	see you soon
à tout à l'heure	see you later
au revoir	goodbye
bonjour	hello, good morning
bonne nuit	good night
bonsoir	good evening, good night
merci	thank you
non	no
oui	yes
pardon	excuse me
peut-être	maybe
s'il te plaît	please (informal)
s'il vous plaît	please (polite or plural)

Useful expressions

Comment dit-on ça en français?
(How do you say that in French?)
Je ne comprends pas.
(I don't understand.)
Je ne sais pas.
(I don't know.)
Je suis désolé(e).
(I'm very sorry.)
Je vous en prie.
(You're welcome.)
Que veut dire ce mot?
(What does this word mean?)

Comment dit-on "it's hot" en français?

On dit "il fait chaud".

La Francophonie

French is not only the language spoken in France. It is also the official language of over 25 countries and is widely spoken in roughly 50 countries and territories worldwide. The French word for the French-speaking world is *la Francophonie*.

France overseas

France is divided up into lots of areas called *départements*, similar to "states" in the US. Some of France's *départements* are not in mainland France but are as far away as South America and the Indian Ocean. These overseas *départements* are known as *départements d'outre-mer* and include Guadeloupe (*la Guadeloupe*), Martinique (*la Martinique*) and Reunion Island (*l'Île de la Réunion*).

French as mother tongue

Your mother tongue is the first language you learn, normally the language spoken in your home. For instance, French is the mother tongue of many people in Switzerland (*la Suisse*), Belgium (*la Belgique*), and *Québec* in Canada.

Canadian French

The French spoken in Canada differs from the French spoken in France in several ways. For a long period of time, French settlers in Canada had little contact with France, so the language didn't evolve in the same way. Some people say Canadian French is more like 16th century French than the French spoken today in France.

Canadian French has been greatly influenced by American English and you may hear phrases such as *c'est le fun* (it's fun) and *avoir un kick sur* (to have an opinion about).

The pronunciation of French also changes from place to place. In Canada, *t* and *d* are pronounced "ts" and "dz" before a *u* or an *i*. So *tu es parti* (you have left) may sound more like "tsu est partsi".

Officially French

Many countries use French as their official language. This means that the main language for running the country is French and that most school lessons are taught in French. For some people, the official language of their country and their mother tongue are quite different. For example, if you live in Senegal, you may speak the main local language - Wolof - at home, but French at school or at work.

French in Africa

French is the official language of the 15 African countries listed below. Some of them have more than one official language: for example, the official languages of Rwanda are French, English and Kinyarwanda.

1 Benin (le Bénin)
2 Burkina-Faso (le Burkina-Faso)
3 Burundi (le Burundi)
4 Chad (le Tchad)
5 Congo, Democratic Republic of the (le Congo-Kinshasa)
6 Congo, Republic of the (le Congo-Brazzaville)
7 Djibouti (Djibouti)
8 Gabon (le Gabon)
9 Guinea (la Guinée)
10 Madagascar (le Madagascar)
11 Mali (le Mali)
12 Niger (le Niger)
13 Rwanda (le Rwanda)
14 Senegal (le Sénégal)
15 Togo (le Togo)

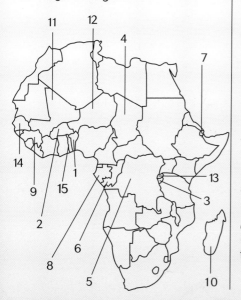

Colorful African expressions

Every language has its own special phrases, or idioms, such as the English phrase "it's raining cats and dogs". In Africa there are many French idioms that are particular to a certain region and do not exist in France. Here are some examples.

In Ivory Coast, a free range chicken is called *un poulet-bicyclette* (a chicken-bicycle) because it is free to use its own feet.

In the Democratic Republic of the Congo, you don't give someone *un pourboire* (a tip), you give them *un tiens-pour-toi* (literally, a "hold for yourself").

Driving in Senegal you might encounter *des tablettes de chocolat*, which translates literally as "some bars of chocolate" but really means "bumpy, pot-holed roads". Meanwhile, in Benin you can say that a man has *une tablette de chocolat*, meaning that he has well-defined chest muscles.

In Mali you have to watch out for *les deux-doigts* (the two-fingers) because that's the local word for "pickpockets".

The French word *becqueter* means "to peck at" but in Burkina Faso the phrase *il t'a bequeté* means someone has shouted at you.

If someone from Ivory Coast says *on a mis papier dans ta tête* (they've put paper in your head) that means you've been educated.

French pronunciation guide

Pronunciation is how words sound. In French, many letters are not said in the same way as in English. French also has groups of letters that are said in a special way.

The list below shows you how letters and groups of letters are usually said. Letters missing from the list sound the same or nearly the same as in English. Bear in mind, though, that there are exceptions and also that people say things differently depending on where they come from.

Learn these tips little by little and try out the words given as examples. If you can get a French speaker to help you, ask them to make the sounds and say the words so that you can copy what you hear.

Vowel sounds

a sounds like "a" in "cat", for example when used in *la*.

e, **eu** and **œu** sound about the same. They sound a bit like the "u" sound in "fur", for example in *je, leur, œuf*. At the end of words that are longer than *je* or *me*, **e** is silent. Before two consonants, **e** usually sounds like **è** (see below), for example in *elle* and *est*.

é sounds a bit like the "a" sound in "late" or the "ai" in "said", for example in *été*.

è, **ê** and **ai** sound like the "ai" sound in "air", for example in *mère, être, aimer*.

i and **y** sound like "ee" in "see", but shorter, for example in *merci, stylo*.

o sounds like "o" in "soft", for example in *port*.

ô, **au** and **eau** sound like "au" in "autumn", for example in *pôle, jaune, bateau;*

ou sounds like "oo" in "mood", for example in *tour*.

oi sounds like "wa" in "wagon", for example in *noir*.

u, as in *tu*, is a sharp "u" sound, but without the "yuh" sound that English puts in front of "u". Round your lips to say "oo", try to say "ee" and you will be close.

ui sounds like the "wee" in "weep", but shorter, for example in *huit*.

Nasal sounds

In French there is a set of slightly nasal sounds written with a vowel + "n" or "m". The sounds are made slightly through the nose as if you had a cold, and without really pronouncing the "n" or "m".

an and **en** are a bit like the "au(n)" sound in "aunt", for example in *blanc, lent*.
am and **em** (when before "b" or "p") sound the same, for example in *chambre, emporter*.

ain and **ein** sound a bit like "a(n)" in "can", for example in *main, plein*.

in sounds like **ain** or **ein** if it is before a consonant or on the end of a word, for example in *magasin, indice.*

im also sounds like **ain** or **ein** if it is before "p" or "b", for example in *impossible.*

on sounds a bit like "o(n)" in "song", for example in *pardon.*

om is the same, for example in *ombre.*

un (on the end of a word or before a consonant) sounds a bit like "an" when you say "an apple", for example in *lundi.*

Consonants

c is hard as in "cat", for example in *sac.* However, before "i" or "e", and when it is written **ç**, it is soft like "s" in "sun", for example in *merci, ça.* The sign that makes a "c" soft is called a cedilla.

ch sounds like "sh" in "shoes", for example in *chat.*

g is pronounced as in "go", for example in *gauche.* However, before "e" or "i" it sounds like the soft "j" sound in "measure", for example in *plage.*

j is said like the "g" in *plage*, for example *jaune.*

gn is like the "nio" sound in "onion", for example in *gagner.*

h is not sounded at all, for example in *heure.*

ll is usually said as in English, but when it follows "i" it sounds like the "y" in "you", for example in *fille.*

A single **l** sometimes sounds the same, particularly when it is after **ai** or **ei** and on the end of a word, for example in *travail* and *soleil.*

qu is the same sound as the hard **c** - like "c" in "cat" - and the "u" is silent, for example in *qui.*

r is a sort of growling "r" sound made in the back of the throat, for example in *mère.*

s sounds like the "z" in "zoo" when it is between two vowels, for example in *trésor.* Otherwise it sounds like "s" in "soap" (the same sound as **ç**), for example in *espérer, sur.*

ss sounds like it is written, for example in *aussi.*

Final consonants

Most consonants are not usually sounded when they are on the end of a word, so *petit* ends in "tee". However, they are often gently sounded if the next word begins with a vowel - so for *un petit ami* you say "a(n) puteetamee".

Many words end in **er**, **et** or **ez**. These all sound just like **é** and the consonant is usually not sounded, for example in *aller, et, cherchez.*

With short words like *les, des* or *mes*, the **es** ending also sounds just like **é**. If words like these come before a vowel, the **s** is sounded like a soft "z", so *les affaires* is pronounced "laizafair". The **x** on the end of *aux* is sounded in just the same way, so *aux autres* sounds like "auzautr".

Speech bubble key: chapters 1 to 5

Chapter 1

- *Luc, regarde!* Luc, look!
- *C'est la côte!* It's the coast!
- *Oh oui! Il y a aussi une ville.* Oh yes! There's a town too.
- *C'est un port.* It's a port.
- *Une rivière!* A river!
- *Un lac!* A lake!
- *Un village!* A village!
- *Oh, des montagnes!* Oh, mountains!
- *Regarde! C'est Tourville.* Look! That's Tourville.
- *Oui, voilà les ponts...* Yes, there are the bridges...
- *...et les deux tours.* ...and the two towers.
- *Oh, voilà l'aéroport.* Oh, there's the airport.
- *Super! Des bonbons.* Great! Candy.
- *Qu'est-ce que c'est, Céline?* What's that, Céline?
- *C'est la carte.* It's the map.
- *Et voici la maison Camembert.* And here's the Camembert house.
- *Oui, voilà la maison.* Yes, there's the house.

Chapter 2

- *J'ai un petit sac noir.* I've got a small black bag.
- *Pst, Luc! Tu as aussi une tente.* Hey, Luc! You've got a tent as well.
- *Ah oui, j'ai une tente verte.* Oh yes, I've got a green tent.
- *Oh, pardon!* Oh, sorry!
- *Oh, il est grand.* Oh, he's tall.
- *Ah... Je suis fatiguée...* Ah... I'm tired...
- *Une valise verte...un sac bleu...* A green suitcase...a blue bag...
- *J'ai un sac vert.* I've got a green bag.
- *Merci. Vous êtes bien gentille.* Thank you. You are so kind.
- *Allô Marion? C'est Céline.* Hello Marion? It's Céline.
- *Nous sommes à Tourville...* We're in Tourville...
- *Non, ça va. Nous avons ta carte.* No, it's alright. We have your map.
- *Mon sac à dos est rouge.* My backpack is red.
- *C'est ton sac.* This is your bag.
- *Mais non, c'est son sac.* No it's not, it's his bag.
- *Mes valises sont grises.* My suitcases are gray.
- *Voici votre valise, Mademoiselle.* Here's your suitcase, Miss.

Chapter 3

- *Tu marches trop lentement.* You're walking too slowly.
- *Mais non, je regarde le paysage.* No I'm not, I'm looking at the countryside.
- *Ah oui, le soleil brille...* Oh yes, the sun's shining...
- *...et les oiseaux chantent.* ...and the birds are singing.
- *Pardon, nous cherchons le camping.* Excuse me, we're looking for the campsite.
- *C'est facile! Vous continuez tout droit.* That's easy! You continue straight ahead.
- *Je veux une table à l'ombre.* I want a table in the shade.
- *Je veux une limonade glacée.* I want an ice-cold lemonade.

- *Je voudrais une limonade.* I'd like a lemonade.
- *Et moi, je voudrais un coca, s'il vous plaît.* And me, I'd like a Coke please.
- *Je voudrais payer, s'il vous plaît.* I'd like to pay, please.
- *Où est mon appareil-photo?* Where's my camera?
- *Nous voulons louer des vélos.* We want to rent some bikes.

The mysterious letter:
A desert island, 1948
My dear son Joseph, I am an old man. I am alone on my desert island and my house near Tourville is empty. I have a secret. I am very wealthy. Now my treasure is your treasure. My house hides the first clue. First of all, you look for the two ships. Farewell, Clément Camembert

Chapter 4

- *Bonjour. Nous sommes les amis de Marion.* Hello. We're Marion's friends.
- *Bonjour. Je suis sa mère.* Hello. I'm her mother.
- *Je m'appelle Aline...et voici notre chien, Toudou.* My name's Aline...and this is our dog, Toudou.
- *À qui est ce chat?* Whose cat is that?
- *Il est à Marion. Il s'appelle Minou.* He's Marion's. His name's Minou.
- *Voici la chambre de mes parents...ma chambre et...la chambre du locataire.* Here's my parents' bedroom...my room and...the lodger's room.
- *Voici ma pièce préférée.* Here's my favorite room.
- *C'est l'atelier de ma mère.* It's my mother's studio.
- *C'est un vieux tableau de la maison Camembert.* That's an old painting of Camembert house.
- *C'est le portrait du grand-père de Marion, Joseph.* That's a portrait of Marion's grandfather, Joseph.
- *Oh non, c'est Mangetout, la chèvre des voisins!* Oh no, it's Mangetout, the neighbors' goat!
- *À qui appartiennent ces vêtements?* Who do these clothes belong to?
- *Ils sont à mon frère...* They're my brother's...
- *Et ces jumelles?* And these binoculars?
- *Elles sont aussi à Luc.* They're Luc's as well.
- *J'aime bien ces lunettes.* I like these glasses.
- *Elles sont à Céline.* They're Céline's.

Chapter 5

- *Attention! Va doucement.* Careful! Go slowly.
- *Reste tranquille, Mangetout.* Keep calm, Mangetout.
- *Lance la corde.* Throw the rope.
- *Sois sage, Toudou.* Be good, Toudou.
- *Fais attention!* Watch out!
- *Allez! Tirez!* Go on! Pull!
- *Fermez vite la barrière, Madame.* Shut the gate quickly!
- *Dépêchez-vous!* Hurry!

Chapters 5 to 9

- *Il faut tout visiter - la vieille église, les grottes, Port-le-Vieux...* You must visit everything - the old church, the caves, Port-le-Vieux...
- *Moi, je dois vite faire des courses à Port-le-Vieux.* I must quickly do some shopping in Port-le-Vieux.
- *À tout à l'heure.* See you later.
- *Il faut fermer la barrière.* You have to shut the gate.
- *Tourne à gauche...et prends le premier chemin à droite.* Turn left...and take the first path on the right.
- *Toudou, viens ici.* Toudou, come here!
- *Ce doit être la maison Camembert.* This must be the Camembert house.
- *Je dois vite trouver cet indice.* I have to find that clue quickly.
- *D'abord, je dois chercher ma lime.* First, I must look for my nail file.
- *Tais-toi!* Be quiet!
- *Ces serrures doivent être très vieilles.* These locks must be very old.

Chapter 6

- *Bonjour Madame Camembert.* Hello Mrs. Camembert.
- *Bonjour Monsieur.* Hello.
- *Est-ce que vous avez des pommes?* Do you have any apples?
- *Avez-vous un panier?* Do you have a basket?
- *Je voudrais deux kilos d'oranges.* I'd like two kilos of oranges.
- *Pourquoi est-ce que la pharmacie est fermée?* Why is the pharmacy closed?
- *Parce que Madame Cachet est malade.* Because Mrs. Cachet is unwell.
- *Pardon, où est la boulangerie?* Excuse me, where is the bakery?
- *Qu'est-ce que c'est?* What's that?
- *C'est un crabe.* It's a crab.
- *Combien coûtent ces gâteaux?* How much do these cakes cost?
- *Combien de croissants voulez-vous?* How many croissants do you want?
- *Qu'est-ce que tu veux?* What do you want?
- *Est-ce que je peux avoir une glace?* Can I have an ice cream?
- *Qu'est-ce que tu cherches, Céline?* What are you looking for Céline?
- *Où est-elle? Ah!* Where is it? Ah!
- *Marion, est-ce que tu peux expliquer cette lettre?* Marion, can you explain this letter?
- *Est-ce que c'est une blague?* Is it a joke?
- *Super! Une vraie chasse au trésor!* Great! A real treasure hunt!

Chapter 7

- *La porte n'est pas fermée à clé...* The door isn't locked.
- *Mais les vélos ne sont pas là.* But the bikes aren't there.
- *Tais-toi, Toudou! Il ne faut pas aboyer si fort!* Be quiet Toudou! You mustn't bark so loud!
- *Qu'est-ce que tu cherches?* What are you looking for?
- *Il n'y a personne...* There isn't anyone here...
- *Il y a un voleur dans la maison!* There's a burglar in the house!
- *Quels bateaux? Je ne trouve pas de bateaux.* What ships? I can't find any ships.
- *Bonsoir chéri. Bonsoir Jean.* Good evening, darling. Good evening, Jean.

- *Bonsoir chérie... Ah non! Il n'y a pas d'aspirines.* Good evening, darling... Oh no! There aren't any aspirins.
- *Oui, je sais. C'est parce que la pharmacie est fermée.* Yes, I know. That's because the pharmacy is closed.
- *Je n'en ai rien, pas d'aspirines, pas de sparadraps...* I haven't got anything, no aspirins, no adhesive bandages...
- *Salut, tout le monde!* Hi, everyone!
- *Oh! Ne regardez pas par ici!* Oh! Don't look over here!
- *Voici les deux bateaux.* Here are the two ships.
- *Oh, il y a un homme dehors.* Oh, there's a man outside.
- *Marion, qui est cet homme?* Marion, who's that man?
- *Je ne sais pas.* I don't know.
- *Ce n'est pas Jean, le locataire...* It's not Jean, the lodger.
- *Où êtes-vous? On dîne!* Where are you? We're eating!
- *OK. On arrive.* OK. We're coming.
- *Regardez! Ils ne sont pas exactement pareils.* Look! They're not exactly the same.

Chapter 8

- *Allons au supermarché, chéri.* Let's go to the supermarket, darling.
- *Attends! Je lis mon journal.* Wait! I'm reading my newspaper.
- *Ton train part bientôt.* Your train's leaving soon.
- *À quelle heure est-ce que tu sors ce soir?* What time are you going out this evening?
- *Ça sent bon...* That smells good...
- *Elle prend du fromage.* She's having cheese.
- *Est-ce que tu prends aussi des frites?* Are you having French fries too?
- *Oh oui, j'adore les frites.* Oh yes, I love French fries.
- *Je ne mange pas de légumes.* I don't eat vegetables.
- *Ces gosses exagèrent! Ils m'agacent!* Those kids are pushing their luck! They're annoying me!
- *Et puis, pourquoi est-ce qu'ils prennent des photos?* And anyhow, why are they taking photos?
- *Attention, il apporte de la soupe.* Watch out, he's bringing some soup.
- *Bon, ça suffit! Sortez tout de suite!* Right, that's enough! Get out this instant!
- *Hep, on part!* Hey, we're going!
- *Hé, regardez! J'ai le prochain indice.* Hey, look! I've got the next clue.

Chapter 9

- *Regardez par la fenêtre.* Look through the window!
- *Près de la sortie...à côté de la femme en rouge.* Near the exit...next to the woman in red.
- *C'est l'homme de l'aéroport!* It's the man from the airport.
- *C'est l'homme avec la lettre!* It's the man with the letter!
- *C'est l'homme du jardin!* It's the man from the garden!
- *C'est le même homme!* It's the same man!
- *Vite! Il doit vouloir notre trésor.* Quickly! He must want our treasure.

Chapters 9 to 12

- *Oh non! L'homme chauve! Là, devant la fontaine.* Oh no! The bald man! There, in front of the fountain.
- *Il vient sur le quai.* He's coming onto the quay.
- *Vite, venez derrière ce filet!* Quick, come behind this net!
- *Ça va!* It's OK!
- *Bon, pose le mot et les photos sur ce banc.* Right, put the note and the photos on this bench.
- *Est-ce que tu as une loupe?* Do you have a magnifying glass?
- *Oui, mais à la maison.* Yes, but at home.
- *Allons chez mon copain, Jérôme. Il habite en face de la gare.* Let's go to my friend Jérôme's. He lives opposite the station.
- *Oui, j'ai une loupe. Elle est sur la table dans le grenier.* Yes, I've got a magnifying glass. It's on the table in the attic.

The note:
The next clue is in a building in Port-le-Vieux. Find the answers to these questions: Where is the dog? Where is the bench? Where is the cow? Where is the farm?

Chapter 10

- *Pourquoi est-ce que vous vous cachez?* Why are you hiding?
- *Parce qu'on n'aime pas l'école.* Because we don't like school.
- *Quelle heure est-il?* What's the time?
- *Il est huit heures, Mademoiselle.* It's eight o'clock, Miss.
- *Et maintenant?* And now?
- *Il est neuf heures et quart.* It's quarter past nine.
- *Gaston, à quelle heure est-ce que tu te lèves?* Gaston, what time do you get up?
- *À sept heures et demie.* At half past seven.
- *Est-ce que tu t'habilles tout seul?* Do you get dressed on your own?
- *Bien sûr.* Of course.
- *Je ne me sens pas bien.* I don't feel well.
- *Bon, calmez-vous!* Right, calm down!
- *Regarde! C'est le crayon qui manque.* Look! It's the crayon that's missing.
- *Hé! C'est mon dessin que tu déchires.* Hey! That's my drawing you're tearing up.
- *Regarde cette vieille photo.* Look at that old photo.
- *Oh! Ce doit être l'indice que nous cherchons.* Oh! That must be the clue we're looking for.
- *C'est Clément Camembert qui coupe le ruban.* That's Clément Camembert cutting the ribbon.
- *Et voilà le signe qui se trouve sur tous ses indices.* And there's the sign that's on all his clues.
- *On peut revenir ce soir.* We can come back this evening.
- *Bonne idée!* Good idea!

Chapter 11

- *Qui êtes vous? Que faites-vous ici?* Who are you? What are you doing here?
- *Euh... Je suis mécanicien. Je suis en train de réparer la photocopieuse.* Er... I'm the mechanic. I'm in the middle of repairing the photocopier.

- *Oui... Je suis en train d'emballer une pièce cassée.* Yes... I'm just wrapping up a broken part.
- *Alors, ça va maintenant?* So it's OK now?
- *Euh, oui...* Er, yes...
- *Est-ce que je peux fermer, Monsieur Vial?* Can I close up, Mr. Vial?
- *Oui, bien sûr.* Yes, of course.
- *Qu'est-ce qu'on fait pour entrer?* What do we do to get in?
- *Venez par ici!* Come this way!
- *Qu'est-ce que tu fais, Céline?* What are you doing, Céline?
- *Ne sois pas bête... Je cherche la photo...* Don't be stupid... I'm looking for the photo...
- *Trop tard! L'homme chauve a l'indice.* Too late! The bald man's got the clue.
- *Comment tu sais ça?* How do you know?
- *Parce que c'est sa serviette.* Because that's his briefcase.
- *Bon, on emporte ça à la gendarmerie.* Right, we're taking this to the police station.
- *C'est fermé!* It's closed!
- *Bon, il faut revenir demain matin.* Right, we must come back tomorrow morning.
- *Est-ce que tu connais le gendarme?* Do you know the policeman?
- *Oui...il est assez sympa.* Yes...he's quite nice.

Chapter 12

- *Qu'est-ce qu'on fait avec la serviette?* What do we do with the briefcase?
- *Est-ce qu'on la montre à tes parents?* Do we show it to your parents?
- *Non, on ne doit pas la leur montrer...* No, we mustn't show it to them...
- *D'abord, on doit tout raconter à la police.* First, we must tell the police everything.
- *On dîne!* We're eating!
- *Je peux la cacher dans ma tente.* I can hide it in my tent.
- *Bonne idée.* Good idea.
- *L'homme chauve a l'indice de l'école.* The bald man's got the clue from the school.
- *Pour le trouver, il faut trouver l'homme chauve.* To find it, we have to find the bald man.
- *Son adresse est peut-être dans sa serviette.* His address might be in his briefcase.
- *Viens à côté de moi.* Come next to me.
- *Céline, passe-lui ma lampe.* Céline, pass her my flashlight.
- *Un agenda, un journal...* A diary, a newspaper...
- *Mais regarde en dessous, il y a des bouts de papier.* But look underneath, there are some pieces of paper.
- *C'est une carte postale en petits morceaux.* It's a postcard in small pieces.
- *Mais est-ce qu'on peut la lire?* But can we read it?

The postcard jigsaw:

Cher Felix, Merci pour ta lettre. Oui, Jules et Emma Champlein habitent près de Tourville. Tu me demandes leur adresse. La voici: la Ferme des Trois Chênes, Route du Pont Neuf, près de Port-le-Vieux. Mais pourquoi Tourville? Ce n'est pas une ville bien passionnante. Enfin, ils ont probablement une chambre pour toi et je te les

recommande. On mange bien chez eux et c'est tranquille.
Alors, bonnes vacances! Nadine

Dear Felix, Thank you for your letter. Yes, Jules and Emma Champlein live near Tourville. You ask me for their address. Here it is: the Trois Chênes farm, Route du Pont Neuf, near Port-le-Vieux. But why Tourville? It's not a very exciting town. Anyhow, they probably have a room for you and I recommend them to you. You eat well at their place and it's quiet. So, have a good trip! Nadine

Chapter 13

- *Alors, où était cette serviette?* So, where was this briefcase?
- *Elle était sur la photocopieuse de l'école.* It was on the school photocopier.
- *Et pourquoi étiez-vous là?* And why were you there?
- *Parce que nous cherchons un trésor...* Because we're looking for treasure...
- *...et il y avait un indice dans l'école.* ...and there was a clue in the school.
- *Quel trésor?* What treasure?
- *Il appartient à ma famille.* It belongs to my family.
- *Ah, je comprends, et cet escroc veut le voler...* Ah, I see, and this crook wants to steal it...
- *Exactement! L'indice est une vieille photo.* Exactly! The clue is an old photo.
- *Hier soir la photo n'était plus là...* Last night the photo wasn't there any more...
- *...mais il y avait la serviette de l'escroc.* ...but the crook's briefcase was there.
- *Elle est très probablement à l'instituteur.* It's most probably the teacher's.
- *Mais non, l'escroc l'avait avant.* But no, the crook had it before.
- *Ça suffit! Rentrez chez vous maintenant.* That's enough! Go home now.
- *Rapportez vite cette serviette à l'école.* Quickly take this briefcase back to school.
- *Tant pis! Il faut continuer sans la police.* Too bad! We must continue without the police.
- *Heureusement, on connaît l'adresse de l'homme chauve.* Luckily we know the bald man's address.
- *Oh, regardez! J'ai toujours l'agenda qui était dans la serviette!* Oh look! I've still got the diary that was in the briefcase!
- *Il était dans ma poche.* It was in my pocket.

Chapter 14

- *Qu'est-ce que c'est?* What's that?
- *C'était dans l'agenda.* It was in the diary.
- *Ça a l'air intéressant...* It looks interesting...

The magazine cutting:

Rare birds on the Wazorare islands
A hundred years ago, there were many blue parrots on the Wazorare islands. The inhabitants worshipped them and built temples to them. These birds are now very rare and it is forbidden to catch any. Last year, you could somtimes see some on Koukou, a more remote desert island.

The message:

Mr. Filou, Find me a pair of blue parrots for my collection.
Your fee: 15,000 euros. Mrs. Hibou.

- *Hé! Les îles Wazorare... Mon arrière-grand-père y allait souvent pour étudier les plantes.* Hey! The Wazorare islands... My great-grandfather often went there to study plants.
- *Il était botaniste...* He was a botanist...
- *Et l'homme chauve était dans ces îles pour voler des perroquets.* And the bald man was on those islands to steal some parrots.
- *Venez, je veux vous montrer quelque chose à la maison.* Come on, I want to show you something at home.

The letter:
Sir, Sadly, your father is very probably dead. He knew our islands well, but at the time of his disappearance he was looking for plants on some dangerous and very remote islands. He was with two botanist friends. They had a good boat, but it was the stormy season. Pedro Paté, Governor of the island

Chapter 15

- *Le déjeuner est presque prêt.* Lunch is almost ready.
- *Est-ce que tu as rapporté du pain?* Did you bring back any bread?
- *Oh pardon, j'ai oublié!* Oh sorry, I forgot!
- *Ça ne fait rien.* It doesn't matter.
- *Il faut attendre Papa... Il va bientôt arriver.* We'll have to wait for Dad... He'll arrive soon.
- *Est-ce que tu as l'agenda?* Have you got the diary?
- *Non, je l'ai mis dans ma tente. Attendez ici!* No, I put it in my tent. Wait here!
- *Oh... Il explique comment il a trouvé la lettre de Clément Camembert.* Oh... It explains how he found Clément Camembert's letter.
- *Il cherchait des perroquets bleus.* He was looking for blue parrots.
- *Il a réussi à atteindre l'île Koukou...* He managed to get to Koukou island...
- *À l'entrée d'une grotte, il a vu un vieux coffre rouillé.* At the entrance to a cave, he saw an old rusty chest.
- *Dedans il a trouvé une lettre qui parlait de trésor.* Inside he found a letter that talked about treasure.
- *Oui, la lettre qu'il a volée...* Yes, the letter that he stole...
- *À table! Voici Papa.* Come and sit down! Here's Dad.
- *Pardon, mais j'ai eu une très longue réunion...* Sorry, but I had a very long meeting...

Chapter 16

- *Il faut aller à la ferme des Trois Chênes...* We must go to the Trois Chênes farm...
- *...pour retrouver Monsieur Filou et l'indice de l'école.* ...to find Mr. Filou and the clue from the school.
- *Du café, Monsieur Filou?* Some coffee, Mr. Filou?
- *Merci... Euh, je voulais vous demander...* Thank you... Er, I wanted to ask you...
- *Je suis allé à Tourville ce matin.* I went to Tourville this morning.
- *J'ai vu le château et les deux tours...* I saw the castle and the two towers...
- *...mais je n'ai pas trouvé la tour en ruine.* ...but I didn't find the ruined tower.

- *Pourquoi voulez-vous la voir? Il y a seulement quelques vieilles pierres.* Why do you want to see it? There are only a few old stones.
- *Euh...j'aime les ruines...* Er...I like ruins...
- *Eh bien, êtes-vous allé au jardin public?* Well, did you go to the park?
- *Oui, mais je n'y ai rien vu.* Yes, but I didn't see anything there.
- *Ah! Vous n'êtes pas descendu jusqu'à la rivière...* Ah! You didn't go right down to the river.
- *Ah Marguerite, tu t'es déjà levée.* Ah Marguerite, you're up already.
- *...Oui, la tour en ruine est au bord de la rivière.* ...Yes, the ruined tower is by the river.
- *Ah, bon... C'est très intéressant.* Oh really... That's very interesting.
- *Le prochain indice doit être à la vieille tour.* The next clue must be at the old tower.

Chapter 17

- *Alors, il a déchiffré l'indice de l'école...* So he's figured out the clue from the school...
- *...qui l'a envoyé à la tour en ruine.* ...which sent him to the ruined tower.
- *Mais il ne l'a pas encore trouvée.* But he hasn't found it yet.
- *Donc nous devons y aller tout de suite - avant lui.* So we must go there right away - before him.
- *On a besoin des vélos.* We need the bikes.
- *Je n'ai jamais vraiment exploré la tour à cause de la clôture.* I've never really explored the tower because of the fence.
- *Rien! J'ai regardé partout et examiné chaque pierre.* Nothing! I've looked everywhere and examined each stone.
- *Eh, j'ai trouvé quelque chose ici!* Hey, I've found something here!
- *Regardez!... C'est le signe de Clément Camembert!* Look!... It's Clément Camembert's sign!

The writing on the tower:
We have kept this ruined tower because it is a sacred monument for the inhabitants of Tourville. The pirates of Pirates' Island destroyed it three years ago, but now, we have got our revenge. We have won our last battle against them, we have expelled them from their fort on the island and they have disappeared from our country.

Chapter 18

- *Alors, il faut aller à l'île des Pirates.* So we must go to Pirates' Island.
- *Pas aujourd'hui. On arrivera trop tard...* Not today. We'll get there too late...
- *Mais l'homme trouvera l'indice ici et...il ira peut-être à l'île pendant la nuit.* But the man will find the clue here and...he might go to the island during the night.
- *Eh bien, il faut cacher cet indice avec des feuilles. Voilà!* Well, we must hide this clue with leaves. There!
- *On peut aussi laisser une fausse piste.* We can also leave a false trail.

- *Génial! Il partira dans la mauvaise direction et ne nous dérangera pas.* Brilliant! He'll go off in the wrong direction and won't disturb us.
- *Bon, il faut lui laisser un mot.* Right, we must leave him a note.
- *J'ai une bonne idée.* I've got a good idea.
- *Mais où est-ce qu'on le cachera?* But where shall we hide it?
- *On peut chercher un bon endroit, Luc et moi.* Luc and I can look for a good place.
- *On peut le cacher ici et dessiner son signe!* We can hide it here and draw his sign!
- *C'est vraiment génial! Il tombera certainement dans le piège.* That's really brilliant! He'll definitely fall for it.

The false trail:

Mon fils, Maintenant tu as trouvé tous les indices que j'ai laissés. Voici ta dernière tâche. Elle sera difficile. Il faudra aller à la gendarmerie de Port-le-Vieux. Tu verras une fenêtre sans barreaux. Tu entreras par là. A l'intérieur, tu trouveras un mur avec des panneaux en bois. Tous mes bijoux et ma fortune seront là. Adieu. C.C.
My son, Now you have found all the clues I left. Here is your last task. It will be difficult. You will have to go to the police station in Port-le-Vieux. You will see one window without bars. You will go in that way. Inside, you will find one wall with wooden panels. All my jewels and my fortune will be there. Farewell. C.C.

Chapter 19

- *Nous allons fermer...* We're going to close up...
- *Très bien. Je partirai bientôt.* Fine. I'll leave soon.
- *Hé, mais c'est l'homme que ces enfants m'ont montré...* Hey, this is the man those children showed me.
- *Oui, c'est le même homme.* Yes it's the same man.
- *Allô Paris? Je voudrais les détails sur le numéro 7454.* Hello Paris? I'd like details on number 7454.
- *Bon, je vais les chercher, puis je vous faxerai.* Right, I'll go and get them and then I'll fax you.
- *Très bien. Merci!* Great. Thanks!
- *Ah, c'est celle-ci. Celles-là ont toutes des barreaux.* Ah, it's this one. Those all have bars.
- *Bon, ce ne sera pas trop difficile. Je pourrai casser la vitre.* Right, it won't be too difficult. I'll be able to break the window pane.
- *D'abord je vais dîner, et je reviendrai quand il fera vraiment nuit.* First I'll go and have supper, and I'll come back when it's really dark.
- *Ah, enfin...* Ah, at last...
- *Bon, demain j'irai à la maison Camembert.* Right, tomorrow I'll go to the Camembert house.
- *Les enfants pourront peut-être m'aider à le trouver.* The children might be able to help me find him.
- *Oh! Qu'est-ce que c'est?* Oh! What's that?
- *C'est lui! Euh... Stop... Je vous arrête.* It's him! Er... Stop... You're under arrest.

Chapters 20 to 22

Chapter 20

- *Est-ce que tu peux me prêter ta serviette?* Can you lend me your towel?
- *Pouah! Elle est aussi mouillée que la mienne.* Yuck! It's as wet as mine.
- *Salut Jérôme! Est-ce que tu as ton bateau ici?* Hi Jérôme! Have you got your boat here?
- *Oui, il est là-bas.* Yes, it's over there.
- *Est-ce qu'on peut l'emprunter? On veut aller à l'île des Pirates.* Can we borrow it? We want to go to Pirates' Island.
- *Oui, bien sûr. C'est le plus petit.* Yes, of course. It's the smallest.
- *Attention, une des rames est plus courte que l'autre...* Watch out, one of the oars is shorter than the other...
- *Eh! On commence à tourner en rond.* Hey! We're starting to go around in circles.
- *Oui, Luc! Tu ne rames pas aussi vite que moi.* Yes, Luc! You're not rowing as fast as me.
- *Tu as la meilleure rame.* You've got the best oar.
- *Mais non, je suis plus forte que toi!* No I haven't, I'm stronger than you!
- *Voilà le fort.* There's the fort.
- *Il est encore plus vieux que la tour en ruine.* It's even older than the ruined tower.
- *Il a plein de cachots et de souterrains...* It's got lots of dungeons and tunnels...
- *...mais on ne peut pas y descendre.* ...but you can't go down there.
- *C'est bizarre, d'habitude la grille est fermée.* That's odd, normally the gate's shut.
- *Eh, allez plus lentement.* Hey, go more slowly.
- *Au secours!* Help!
- *Regardez, il y a quatre souterrains.* Look, there are four tunnels.
- *Oh non...* Oh no...
- *On ne peut plus sortir!* We can't get out any more!
- *Venez ici! Regardez ça!* Come here! Look at this!
- *Mon souterrain n'est pas aussi long que le tien.* My tunnel isn't as long as yours.
- *Mon premier souterrain était aussi long que le tien, mais mon deuxième est plus court.* My first tunnel was as long as yours, but my second one is shorter.
- *Le mien est plus long que le premier de Céline.* Mine is longer than Céline's first one.

Chapter 21

- *Si le trésor est ici, on le trouvera!* If the treasure is here, we'll find it!
- *Rien! Le souterrain se termine ici.* Nothing! The tunnel ends here.
- *Est-ce que tu verrais mieux si tu avais la lampe?* Would you see better if you had the flashlight?
- *Oui, passe-la-moi!* Yes, pass it to me!
- *Oh, il y a un anneau en fer dans le mur! Je vais tirer dessus.* Oh, there's an iron ring in the wall! I'm going to give it a pull.
- *Oh là!* Wow!
- *Bonjour, je voudrais parler à Marion, Luc et Céline.* Hello, I'd like to talk to Marion, Luc and Céline.
- *Je voudrais les remercier. Ils m'ont aidé à attraper un escroc!* I'd like to thank them. They helped me to catch a crook!
- *Aimeriez-vous les attendre?* Would you like to wait for them?

- *Non, je reviendrai. Je ne voudrais pas vous déranger.* No, I'll come back. I wouldn't want to disturb you.
- *Mais d'abord vous pourriez peut-être nous raconter l'histoire. Nous n'en savons rien!* But first you could perhaps tell us the story. We know nothing about it!

Chapter 22

- *Bon... On devrait chercher une sortie.* Right... We should look for a way out.
- *On en trouvera peut-être une si on retourne aux marches.* We might find one if we go back to the steps.
- *Regardez! De la lumière!* Look! Light!
- *Ouf!* Whew!
- *Céline, si tu bouges ces pierres, personne ne pourra voir l'entrée.* Céline, if you move those rocks, nobody'll be able to see the entrance.
- *Je vais pouvoir offrir une nouvelle paire de rames à Jérôme!* I'm going to be able to treat Jérôme to a new pair of oars!

Marion's letter:
Monday, September 2
Dear Luc and Céline, Here's the article from the Tourville Echo that tells our story. It's brilliant! What are you going to do with your share of the reward? I'm going to buy a CD player with mine. If your Mom agrees, I'll come to your place during the Christmas holidays, so see you soon I hope! Love, Marion

The newspaper article:
The Camembert family treasure.

Marion Camembert with her friends Luc and Céline Meunier and her dog, Toudou. Félix Filou, the rare bird thief who wanted to steal the Camembert family treasure.

For Marion Camembert and her friends Luc and Céline, August has been an exciting month. They found some treasure and helped the police to catch a crook, Félix Filou.

A few months ago, Filou was on one of the Wazorare islands. He was looking for some very rare parrots there that he wanted to steal. He came across a letter from Clément, Marion's great-grandfather. It was an old letter addressed to Joseph, Marion's grandfather, and left on the island in an old chest after Clément's death. The letter was the first clue in a treasure hunt. It brought Filou to Tourville where, stupidly, he lost it. Luc and Céline, who were coming to spend a few days with their friend Marion, found it. The three teenagers managed to find the treasure (gold), hidden in the old Pirates' Fort, before the crook, and they helped the police to catch him.

The three heroes also received a reward of 2,000 euros from the police. Our congratulations to them!

Common irregular verbs: a - e

Here is a table listing the main irregular French verbs in this book, in alphabetical order. The first column shows the infinitive of the verb, followed by the three different imperatives (*tu, nous* and *vous* forms), then the past participle (p.p.). To make the perfect tense you take the present tense of *avoir* or *être* plus the past participle. If a verb takes *être* in the perfect tense, then it will say "with *être*" after the past participle.

	Present tense	Imperfect tense	Future tense
acheter (to buy)	j'achète	j'achetais	j'achèterai
	tu achètes	tu achetais	tu achèteras
achète! achetons!	il/elle achète	il/elle achetait	il/elle achètera
achetez!	nous achetons	nous achetions	nous achèterons
	vous achetez	vous achetiez	vous achèterez
past participle: acheté	ills/elles achètent	ils/elles achetaient	ils/elles achèteront
aller (to go)	je vais	j'allais	j'irai
	tu vas	tu allais	tu iras
va! allons! allez!	il/elle va	il/elle allait	il/elle ira
	nous allons	nous allions	nous irons
p.p. allé (with être)	vous allez	vous alliez	vous irez
	ils/elles vont	ils/elles allaient	ils/elles iront
appeler (to call)	j'appelle	j'appelais	j'appellerai
	tu appelles	tu appelais	tu appelleras
appelle! appelons!	il/elle appelle	il/elle appelait	il/elle appellera
appelez!	nous appelons	nous appelions	nous appellerons
	vous appelez	vous appeliez	vous appellerez
p.p. appelé	ils/elles appellent	ils/elles appelaient	ils/elles appelleront
avoir (to have)	j'ai	j'avais	j'aurai
	tu as	tu avais	tu auras
aie! ayons! ayez!	il/elle a	il/elle avait	il/elle aura
	nous avons	nous avions	nous aurons
p.p. eu	vous avez	vous aviez	vous aurez
	ils/elles ont	ils/elles avaient	ils/elles auront
boire (to drink)	je bois	je buvais	je boirai
	tu bois	tu buvais	tu boiras
bois! buvons! buvez!	il/elle boit	il/elle buvait	il/elle boira
	nous buvons	nous buvions	nous boirons
p.p. bu	vous buvez	vous buviez	vous boirez
	ils/elles boivent	ils/elles buvaient	ils/elles boiront
connaître (to know)	je connais	je connaissais	je connaîtrai
	tu connais	tu connaissais	tu connaîtras
connais! connaissons!	il/elle connaît	il/elle connaissait	il/elle connaîtra
connaissez!	nous connaissons	nous connaissions	nous connaîtrons
	vous connaissez	vous connaissiez	vous connaîtrez
p.p. connu	ils/elles connaissent	ils/elles connaissaient	ils/elles connaîtront

	Present tense	Imperfect tense	Future tense
devoir (to have to)	je dois	je devais	je devrai
	tu dois	tu devais	tu devras
dois! devons! devez!	il/elle doit	il/elle devait	il/elle devra
	nous devons	nous devions	nous devrons
p.p. dû	vous devez	vous deviez	vous devrez
	ils/elles doivent	ils/elles devaient	ils/elles devront
dire (to say)	je dis	je disais	je dirai
	tu dis	tu disais	tu diras
dis! disons! dites!	il/elle dit	il disait	il/elle dira
	nous disons	nous disions	nous dirons
p.p. dit	vous dites	vous disiez	vous direz
	ils/elles disent	ils/elles disaient	ils/elles diront
dormir (to sleep)	je dors	je dormais	je dormirai
	tu dors	tu dormais	tu dormiras
dors! dormons!	il/elle dort	il/elle dormait	il/elle dormira
dormez!	nous dormons	nous dormions	nous dormirons
	vous dormez	vous dormiez	vous dormirez
p.p. dormi	ils/elles dorment	ils/elles dormaient	ils/elles dormiront
écrire (to write)	j'écris	j'écrivais	j'écrirai
	tu écris	tu écrivais	tu écriras
écris! écrivons!	il/elle écrit	il/elle écrivait	il/elle écrira
écrivez!	nous écrivons	nous écrivions	nous écrirons
	vous écrivez	vous écriviez	vous écrirez
p.p. écrit	ils/elles écrivent	ils/elles écrivaient	ils/elles écriront
espérer (to hope)	j'espère	j'espérais	j'espérerai
	tu espères	tu espérais	tu espéreras
espère! espérons!	il/elle espère	il/elle espérait	il/elle espérera
espérez!	nous espérons	nous espérions	nous espérerons
	vous espérez	vous espériez	vous espérerez
p.p. espéré	ils/elles espèrent	ils/elles espéraient	ils/elles espéreront
essayer (to try)	j'essaie	j'essayais	j'essaierai
	tu essaies	tu essayais	tu essaieras
essaie! essayons!	il/elle essaie	il/elle essayait	il/elle essaiera
essayez!	nous essayons	nous essayions	nous essaierons
	vous essayez	vous essayiez	vous essaierez
p.p. essayé	ils/elles essaient	ils/elles essayaient	ils/elles essaieront
être (to be)	je suis	j'étais	je serai
	tu es	tu étais	tu seras
sois! soyons! soyez!	il/elle est	il/elle était	il/elle sera
	nous sommes	nous étions	nous serons
p.p. été	vous êtes	vous étiez	vous serez
	ils/elles sont	ils/elles étaient	ils/elles seront

Common irregular verbs: f - v

	Present tense	**Imperfect tense**	**Future tense**
faire **(to do, make)**	je fais	je faisais	je ferai
	tu fais	tu faisais	tu feras
	il/elle fait	il/elle faisait	il/elle fera
fais! faisons! faites!	nous faisons	nous faisions	nous ferons
	vous faites	vous faisiez	vous ferez
p.p. *fait*	ils font	ils/elles faisaient	ils/elles feront
se lever **(to get up)**	je me lève	je me levais	je me lèverai
	tu te lèves	tu te levais	tu te lèveras
lève-toi! levons-nous!	il/elle se lève	il/elle se levait	il/elle se lèvera
levez-vous!	nous nous levons	nous nous levions	nous nous lèverons
	vous vous levez	vous vous leviez	vous vous lèverez
p.p. *levé* (with *être*)	ils/elles se lèvent	ils/elles se levaient	ils/elles lèveront
lire **(to read)**	je lis	je lisais	je lirai
	tu lis	tu lisais	tu liras
lis! lisons! lisez!	il/elle lit	il/elle lisait	il/elle lira
	nous lisons	nous lisions	nous lirons
p.p. *lu*	vous lisez	vous lisiez	vous lirez
	ils/elles lisent	ils/elles lisaient	ils/elles liront
mettre **(to put)**	je mets	je mettais	je mettrai
	tu mets	tu mettais	tu mettras
mets! mettons!	il/elle met	il/elle mettait	il/elle mettra
mettez!	nous mettons	nous mettions	nous mettrons
	vous mettez	vous mettiez	vous mettrez
p.p. *mis*	ils/elles mettent	ils/elles mettaient	ils/elles mettront
ouvrir **(to open)**	j'ouvre	j'ouvrais	j'ouvrirai
	tu ouvres	tu ouvrais	tu ouvriras
ouvre! ouvrons!	il/elle ouvre	il/elle ouvrait	il/elle ouvrira
ouvrez!	nous ouvrons	nous ouvrions	nous ouvrirons
	vous ouvrez	vous ouvriez	vous ouvrirez
p.p. *ouvert*	ils/elles ouvrent	ils/elles ouvraient	ils/elles ouvriront
partir **(to leave)**	je pars	je partais	je partirai
	tu pars	tu partais	tu partiras
pars! partons! partez!	il/elle part	il/elle partait	il/elle partira
	nous partons	nous partions	nous partirons
p.p. *parti* (with *être*)	vous partez	vous partiez	vous partirez
	ils/elles partent	ils/elles partaient	ils/elles partiront
pouvoir **(can, to be able to)**	je peux	je pouvais	je pourrai
	tu peux	tu pouvais	tu pourras
	il/elle peut	il/elle pouvait	il/elle pourra
no imperatives	nous pouvons	nous pouvions	nous pourrons
	vous pouvez	vous pouviez	vous pourrez
p.p. *pu*	ils/elles peuvent	ils/elles pouvaient	ils/elles pourront

	Present tense	Imperfect tense	Future tense
prendre (to take)	je prends	je prenais	je prendrai
	tu prends	tu prenais	tu prendras
prends! prenons!	il/elle prend	il/elles prenait	il/elle prendra
prenez!	nous prenons	nous prenions	nous prendrons
	vous prenez	vous preniez	vous prendrez
p.p. *pris*	ils/elles prennent	ils/elles prenaient	ils/elles prendront
recevoir (to receive)	je reçois	je recevais	je recevrai
	tu reçois	tu recevais	tu recevras
reçois! recevons!	il/elle reçoit	il/elle recevait	il/elle recevra
recevez!	nous recevons	nous recevions	nous recevrons
	vous recevez	vous receviez	vous recevrez
p.p. *reçu*	ils/elles reçoivent	ils/elles recevaient	ils/elles recevront
savoir (to know)	je sais	je savais	je saurai
	tu sais	tu savais	tu sauras
sache! sachons!	il/elle sait	il/elle savait	il/elle saura
sachez!	nous savons	nous savions	nous saurons
	vous savez	vous saviez	vous saurez
p.p. *su*	ils/elles savent	ils/elles savaient	ils/elles sauront
sortir (to go out)	je sors	je sortais	je sortirai
	tu sors	tu sortais	tu sortiras
sors! sortons! sortez!	il/elle sort	il/elle sortait	il/elle sortira
	nous sortons	nous sortions	nous sortirons
p.p. *sorti* (with *être*)	vous sortez	vous sortiez	vous sortirez
	ils/elles sortent	ils/elles sortaient	ils/elles sortiront
venir (to come)	je viens	je venais	je viendrai
	tu viens	tu venais	tu viendras
viens! venons! venez!	il/elle vient	il/elle venait	il/elle viendra
	nous venons	nous venions	nous viendrons
p.p. *venu* (with *être*)	vous venez	vous veniez	vous viendrez
	ils/elles viennent	ils/elles venaient	ils/elles viendront
voir (to see)	je vois	je voyais	je verrai
	tu vois	tu voyais	tu verras
vois! voyons! voyez!	il/elle voit	il/elle voyait	il/elle verra
	nous voyons	nous voyions	nous verrons
p.p. *vu*	vous voyez	vous voyiez	vous verrez
	ils/elles voient	ils/elles voyaient	ils/elles verront
vouloir (to want)	je veux	je voulais	je voudrai
	tu veux	tu voulais	tu voudras
veuille! veuillons!	il/elle veut	il/elle voulait	il/elle voudra
veuillez!	nous voulons	nous voulions	nous voudrons
	vous voulez	vous vouliez	vous voudrez
p.p. *voulu*	ils/elles veulent	ils/elles voulaient	ils/elles voudront

Vocabulary list: a - c

ere is a list of the French words used in this book, along with their English translations.

Nouns

If a noun has **l'** or **les** in front of it, its gender (masculine **[m]** or feminine **[f]** will be shown after it. Nouns with irregular plurals have their plural ending in brackets. Add the letter(s) in brackets to the noun to get the plural form:
e.g. **l'anneau(x) [m]** is masculine and its plural is **les anneaux**. If the plural form is very different, it is given in full in brackets.

Adjectives

To make the feminine form of an adjective, add the letter(s) in brackets to the end of the word: e.g. **bon(ne)** becomes **bonne**. If the feminine form is very different, it is given in full in brackets.

Verbs

An asterisk (*) after a verb indicates it is irregular. The most common irregular verbs are conjugated on pages 112-115.

A

à	in, at, to
à bientôt	see you soon
à cause de	because of
à côté de	next to
à droite	(to/on the) right
à gauche	(to/on the) left
à l'intérieur	inside
à la maison	(at) home
à l'ombre	in the shade
à quelle heure?	what time?
à qui?	whose?, to who(m)?
à toute à l'heure	see you later
à travers	through
abandonner	to abandon, to leave
aboyer*	to bark
acheter*	to buy
adieu	farewell
l'adolescent [m]	teenager
adorer	to adore, to love
l'adresse [f]	address
adresser	to address
l'aéroport [m]	airport
les affaires [f]	things
l'Afrique [f]	Africa
africain(e)	African
s'agacer	to annoy, bother
l'agenda [m]	diary
aider	to help
aimer	to like, to love
l'Allemagne [f]	Germany
l'allemand [m]	German (language)
aller*	to go
amitiés	love (from)

(bien) s'amuser	to have (lots of) fun
allô	hello (used on phone)
alors	then, so, well
l'Amérique [f]	America
l'ami [m], l'amie [f]	friend
l'an [m], l'année [f]	year
l'Angleterre [f]	England
l'anneau(x) [m]	ring
...ans	...years old
l'appareil-photo	camera
appartenir* à	to belong to
apporter	to bring
apprendre*	to learn
après	after
après-demain	the day after tomorrow
l'arbre [m]	tree
l'argent [m]	money
arrêter	to stop, to arrest
l'arrière-grand-père [m]	great-grandfather
arriver	to arrive, to happen
l'article [m]	article
l'Asie [f]	Asia
l'aspirine [f]	aspirin
assez	quite
assez de/d'	enough
l'atelier [m]	studio
atteindre*	to reach, to get to
attendre*	to wait
attention	watch out, careful
attraper	to catch
au bord de/d'	by (the side of)
au bout de/d'	at/to the end

aujourd'hui	today
aussi	too, also, as well, (just) as
aussi...que/qu'	as...as
l'Australasie [f]	Australasia
l'Australie [f]	Australia
autre	other, another
l'Autriche [f]	Austria
avant	before
avant-hier	the day before yesterday
avec	with
avoir*	to have
avoir* besoin de/d'	to need
avoir* l'air	to look, to appear, to seem

B

(gros) baisers [m]	(lots of) kisses
le ballon	ball
le banc	bench
le barreau(x)	bar (on window)
la barrière	gate
les baskets [f]	tennis shoes
la bataille	battle
le bateau(x)	ship, boat
le bâtiment	building
bâtir	to build
beau/bel (belle)	beautiful, handsome
beaucoup de/d'	many, a lot of
bête	stupid, silly
bêtement	stupidly
bien	well, very, most, really, so
bien sûr	of course
bientôt	soon
le bijou(x)	piece of jewelry
le billet	ticket
la bise	kiss
bizarre	weird, strange, odd
la blague	joke
blanc(he)	white
bleu(e)	blue
le bois	wood
bon(ne)	good, right, nice
le bonbon	candy
bonjour	hello
bonnes vacances	(have a) good trip
bonsoir	good evening/night
le/la botaniste	botanist
les bottes [f]	boots
bouger	to move
la bougie	candle
la boulangerie	bakery
le bout	piece
briller	to shine
le bruit	noise

C

ça	this, that
ça ne fait rien	it doesn't matter
ça suffit	that's enough
ça va	(it's) all right
cacher	to hide
se cacher	to hide (yourself)
le cachot	dungeon
le café	café, coffee
se calmer	to calm down
le camembert	camembert (a French cheese)
le camping	camping
le Canada	Canada
le carrefour	junction
la carte	map
la carte (à jouer)	(playing) card
la carte postale	postcard
le carton	(cardboard) box
cassé(e)	broken
casser	to break (something)
se casser	to break
ce, c'	this
ce/cet, cette (ces)	this (those)
ce matin	this morning
ce sont	they/these/those are
ceci, cela	this, that
la chambre	(bed)room
le champ	field
changer	to change
la chanson	song
chanter	to sing
le chapeau(x)	hat
le chapeau(x) haut de forme	top hat
chaque	each
la chasse au trésor	treasure hunt
chasser	to chase (away)
le chat	cat
le château(x)	castle
chaud(e)	warm
la chaussette	sock
la chaussure	shoe
chauve	bald
le chemin	path, lane, way
la chemise	shirt
cher (chère)	dear, expensive
chercher	to look for
chéri [m], chérie [f]	darling, dear
les cheveux [m]	hair
la chèvre	goat
chez	at the house of, at ...'s
chez moi/toi, etc.	at my/your, etc. place
le chien	dog
choisir	to choose
le ciel	sky

Vocabulary list: c - i

le cinéma	movie theatre	descendre*	to go down(stairs)
la clé	key	désert(e)	deserted, desert
la clôture	fence	désirer	to wish
le coca	Coke	le dessin	drawing
le coffre	chest (container)	dessiner	to draw
le coffre-fort	safe	dessus	on top of (it), on (it)
le collant	tights	le détail	detail
la collection	collection	détruire*	to destroy
la colline	hill	deux	two
combien (de + noun)	how much, how many	deuxième	second
comme	as, like	devant	in front of
comment	how	devenir*	to become
comprendre*	to understand	devoir*	to have to, must
connaître*	to know	d'habitude	usually, normally
content(e)	pleased, happy	difficile	difficult
continuer	to continue	dîner	to have supper
contre	against	le dîner	supper
le copain, la copine	good friend	la direction	direction
la corde	rope	disparaître*	to disappear
le costume	suit	la disparition	disappearance
la côte	coast	donc	so, therefore
se coucher	to go to bed	dormir*	to sleep, to be asleep
couper	to cut	doucement	slowly
le couple	couple, pair	droite	right
couramment	fluently	du, de la, de l', des	some, any, of the
court(e)	short		
coûter	to cost	**E**	
le crabe	crab		
le crayon (de couleur)	crayon	l'eau [f]	water
la croisière	cruise, crossing	l'écho [m]	echo
le croissant	croissant	l'école [f]	school
		l'église [f]	church
D		elle	she, it
		elles	they
d'abord	first of all	éloigné(e)	remote, far away
dangereux	dangerous	emballer	to wrap (up)
(dangereuse)		emporter	to take (away)
dans	in, into	emprunter	to borrow
danser	to dance	en	in (before a language,
de/d'	of, from		month, etc.), some, an
de temps en temps	sometimes	en dessous	underneath
le dé	die (plural: dice)	en face de	opposite
déchiffrer	to decipher	en retard	late
déchirer	to tear (up)	en ruine	ruined, in ruins
dedans	inside	encore	even, again, more
dehors	outside	l'endroit [m]	place
déjà	already	l'enfant [m]	child
le déjeuner	lunch	enfin	at last, anyhow
demain	tomorrow	entendre	to hear
demain matin	tomorrow morning	entre	between
demander	to ask	l'entrée [f]	entrance
se dépêcher	to hurry (up)	entrer	to go in/enter/come in
dépenser	to spend	envoyer*	to send
déranger	to disturb	l'escroc [m]	crook
dernier (dernière)	last	espérer	to hope
derrière	behind	et	and
dès que/qu'	as soon as	et puis	and then, and also

les États-Unis [m]	United States
l'été [m]	summer
être*	to be
être* d'accord	to agree
étudier	to study
l'euro [m]	euro
exactement	exactly
exagérer	to exaggerate, to go too far
examiner	to examine
l'excursion [f]	outing, trip
expliquer	to explain
explorer	to explore

F

facile	easy
faire*	to do, to make
faire* attention	to watch out, to be careful
faire* des courses	to go shopping
faire* de la cuisine	to do the cooking
faire* nuit	to be night-time/dark
faire* des randonnées	to go hiking
faire* du ski	to go skiing
la famille	family
fantastique	fantastic
fatigué(e)	tired
faux (fausse)	false
faxer	to fax, to send a fax
féliciter	to congratulate
la femme	woman
la fenêtre	window
le fer	iron
la ferme	farm
fermé(e) à clé	locked
fermer	to close, to shut
la fête	party, festival, feast
la feuille	leaf
les feux [m]	traffic lights
le filet	net
la fille	girl, daughter
le fils	son
finir	to finish
la fontaine	fountain
la forêt	forest
fort(e)	loud(ly)
le fort	fort
la fortune	fortune
la fraise	strawberry
le français	French (language)
la France	France
le frère	brother
les frites [f]	French fries
le fromage	cheese

G

gagner	to win, to earn
le garçon	boy
garder	to keep
la gare	station
le gâteau(x)	cake
gauche	left
le gendarme	policeman
la gendarmerie	police station
génial(e)	brilliant
gentil(le)	kind, nice
la géographie	geography
la glace	ice cream
glacé(e)	ice-cold
le gosse	kid
goûter	to taste, to have a taste
le gouverneur	governor
la grand-mère	grandmother
le grand-père	grandfather
grand(e)	big, large, tall
la (grande) route	(main) road
le grenier	attic
la grille	gate
gris(e)	gray
gros(se)	big, large, fat
la grotte	cave
le guide	guide, guidebook

H

s'habiller	to dress, to get dressed
l'habitant [m]	inhabitant
habiter	to live
l'herbe [f]	grass
le héros	hero
l'heure [f]	hour
...heures	...o'clock
heureusement	luckily, happily
hier	yesterday
hier soir	yesterday evening
l'histoire [f]	history, story
l'homme [m]	man
hors de	out of
l'hôtel [m]	hotel
huit	eight

I

ici	here
l'idée [f]	idea
il	he/it
il est interdit de/d'	it is forbidden to
il faut	it is necessary to
il pleut	it's raining
il s'appelle	his/its name is

Vocabulary list: i - p

il y a	there is/are, ago
l'île [f]	island
ils	they
impossible	impossible
l'indice [m]	clue
s'inquiéter	to worry
l'instituteur [m],	(elementary school)
l'institutrice [f]	teacher
l'Irlande [f]	Ireland
l'Italie [f]	Italy
intelligent(e)	intelligent
intéressant(e)	interesting

J

jamais	never (not ever)
le Japon	Japan
le jardin	garden, back yard
le jardin public	park
jaune	yellow
je, j'	I
je m'appelle	my name is
le jean	jeans
joli(e)	pretty
le jour, la journée	day
le journal (journaux)	newspaper
les jumelles [f]	binoculars
la jupe	skirt
le jus d'orange	orange juice
jusqu'à	as far as, up/down to, until

K

le kilo (de/d'...)	kilo of

L

là	there
là-bas	over there
le lac	lake
laisser	to leave (behind)
laisser tomber	to drop
la lampe (de poche)	flashlight
lancer	to throw
se laver	to bathe
le, la, l', les	the
le lecteur de CD	CD player
le légume	vegetable
lent(e)	slow
lentement	slowly
la lettre	letter
se lever	to get up
libre	free
la lime	nail file
la limonade	lemonade

lire*	to read
le livre	book
le locataire	lodger
loin de	far from
long(ue)	long
lors de	at the time of
louer	to rent
la loupe	magnifying glass
la lumière	light
la lune	moon
lundi	Monday
les lunettes [f]	glasses

M

Madame	Mrs.
Mademoiselle	Miss
le magasin	shop
le magicien	magician
la main	hand
maintenant	now
le maire	mayor
mais	but
la maison	house
mal	badly
malade	sick
malheureusement	unfortunately
Maman	Mom, Mommy
manger	to eat
manquer	to be missing
le manteau(x)	coat
la marche	step
le marché	market
marcher	to walk
mardi	Tuesday
le mari	husband
marron	brown
la matière	subject
mauvais(e)	wrong, bad
le mécanicien	mechanic
meilleur(e)	better
le/la/les meilleur(e)(s)	the best
le/la/les même(s)	the same
mener	to lead
mentir*	to lie (tell lies)
la mer	the sea
merci	thank you
la mère	mother
le métro	underground (railway)
mettre*	to put
mettre* de l'ordre	to straighten up
midi	noon
mieux	better
le mieux	the best
le ministre	(government) minister
minuit	midnight
moche	horrible, ugly

moi	me, as for me
moins	fewer/less
le moins	fewest/least
le mois	month
Monsieur (Messieurs)	Mr., sir
la montagne	mountain
monter	to go up(stairs)
montrer	to show
le monument	monument
le morceau(x)	piece
mort(e)	dead
la mort	death
le mot	word, note
la moto	motorcycle
mouillé(e)	wet
mourir	to die
le mur	wall
le musée	museum

N

naître	to be born
ne...jamais	not...ever
ne...pas	not
ne...pas de/d'	not a, not any, no
ne...pas encore	not yet
ne...personne	not...anybody, nobody
ne...plus	not any more
ne...rien	not...anything, nothing
neuf (neuve)	(brand) new
Noël	Christmas
noir(e)	black
non	no
nous	we
nouveau/nouvel(le)	new
les nouvelles [f]	news
la nuit	night
le numéro	number

O

l'objet [m]	object, thing
l'œuf [m] (œufs)	egg
offrir*	to give, to offer
oh là!	oh no!, oh dear!
l'oiseau(x) [m]	bird
l'ombre [f]	shade, shadow
on	we, one, you
l'or [m]	gold
l'orange [f]	orange
l'ordinateur [m]	computer
l'oreille [f]	ear
où	where
oublier	to forget
oui	yes
l'outil [m]	tool
ouvrir*	to open

P

le pain	bread
la paire	pair
le panier	basket
par	by, through (a window)
par ici	this way, over here
par là	that way, over there
le parasol	parasol
parce que	because
pardon	sorry, excuse me
pareil(le)	(the) same
les parents [m]	parents
parfait(e)	perfect
parfois	sometimes
le parfum	flavor, perfume
parler	to speak
la part	part, share
partir*	to go (away), to leave
partout	everywhere
pas	not
le passage clouté	pedestrian crossing
passer	to pass, to spend (time)
passionnant(e)	exciting
payer*	to pay
le pays	country
le Pays de Galles	Wales
le paysage	countryside
pendant	during
penser	to think
perdre*	to lose
le père	father
le perroquet	parrot
personne	nobody
petit(e)	small, little, short
peu	few, little
peut-être	perhaps
la pharmacie	pharmacy
la photo	photo
la photocopieuse	photocopier
la pièce	room, part
le piège	trap
la pierre	rock, stone
le pirate	pirate
pire	worse
le/la/les pire(s)	the worst
la piscine	swimming pool
la piste	trail
la plage	beach
la plante	plant
plein(e)	full
plein de/d'	lots of
pleuvoir*	to rain
la pluie	rain
plus	more
le/la/les plus	the most
la poche	pocket

Vocabulary list: p - y

le pôle	pole
la police	police
la pomme	apple
le pont	bridge
le port	port
la porte	door
porter	to carry, to wear
le portrait	portrait
poser	to put down
la poste	post office
pour	for, in order to, to
pourquoi	why
pouvoir*	to be able to, can, may
préféré(e)	favorite
(le) premier, (la) première	(the) first
prendre*	to take
(tout) près de	(right) near
presque	almost, nearly
prêt(e)	ready
prêter	to lend
probablement	probably
prochain(e)	next
le propriétaire	owner, landlord
le professeur/prof	teacher
le pull	jumper

Q

le quai	quay, platform
quand	when
quatrième	fourth
que (qu')	who(m), which, what, than
quel(le)	which, what
quelle heure est-il?	what time is it?
quelque chose	something
quelque part	somewhere
quelques	a few
qu'est-ce que (c'est)?	what (is it/this/that)?
la question	question
qui	who, which

R

raconter	to tell
ramasser	to pick up
la rame	oar
ramer	to row (a boat)
ranger	to put away
rapporter	to bring/take back
se raser	to shave
recevoir*	to receive, to get
recherché(e)	sought after, wanted
recommander	to recommend

la récompense	reward
reconnaître*	to recognize
réfléchir	to think
regarder	to look at
regretter	to regret
remercier	to thank
rentrer	to come/go (back/home)
réparer	to repair, to mend
la réponse	answer
réserver	to reserve
le restaurant	restaurant
rester	to stay, to remain
retourner	to go back
retrouver	to track down
la réunion	meeting
réussir (à)	to manage (to), to succeed (in)
se réveiller	to wake up
revenir*	to come back, to return
riche	rich, wealthy
rien	nothing
la rivière	river
la robe	dress
rose	pink
rouge	red
rouillé(e)	rusty
la route	road
le ruban	ribbon
la rue	street
la ruine	ruin

S

le sac	bag
le sac à dos	backpack
sacré(e)	sacred
sage	well behaved, good
le salaire	pay, salary, fee
salut	hi, hello, bye
savoir*	to know
le secours	help
le secret	secret
sentir*	to feel, to smell
se sentir* bien/mal	to feel well/ill
la serrure	lock
la serviette	briefcase, towel
servir*	to serve
seul(e)	alone
seulement	only
le short	shorts
si	so, if
le signe	sign
s'il te/vous plaît	please
la sœur	sister
le soir, la soirée	evening
le soleil	sun
la sortie	exit

sortir*	to go out	trop	too
la soupe	soup	trouver	to find
sous	under	se trouver	to be found/situated
le souterrain	underground passage	tu	you
souvent	often		
le sparadrap	adhesive bandage		
le sport	sport	**U**	
suivre*	to follow		
super, superbe	great, gorgeous	un(e)	a, an, one
le supermarché	supermarket		
sur	on, onto	**V**	
le sweat-shirt	sweatshirt		
sympa(tique)	nice	les vacances [f]	vacation
		la vache	cow
T		la valise	suitcase
la table	table	la vallée	valley
le tableau(x)	painting	le vélo	bike
la tâche	task	vénérer	to worship
se taire*	to be quiet	se venger	to get revenge
tant pis	too bad	venir*	to come
la tante	aunt	vers	towards
tard	late	vert(e)	green
le tee-shirt	T-shirt	la veste	jacket
téléphoner	to telephone	les vêtements [m]	clothes
la tempête	storm	vide	empty
le temple	temple	vieux/vieil (vieille)	old
tenir*	to hold	le village	village
la tente	tent	la ville	town
se terminer	to end, to finish	visiter	to visit
le terrain de camping	campsite	vite	quickly, fast
la terre	earth, soil	la vitre	window pane
le thé	tea	voici	here's, here are
tirer	to pull	voilà	there's, there are
le toit	roof	voir*	to see
tomber	to fall (over)	le voisin	neighbor
tomber dans la piège	to fall in the trap	la voiture	car
tomber sur	to find by chance	le vol	theft
toujours	always, still	voler	to steal, to rob
la tour	tower	le voleur	burglar, thief
tourner	to turn	vouloir*	to want
tourner en rond	to go around in circles	vous	you
tout	everything	vrai(e)	true, real
tout de suite	right away, this instant	vraiment	really
tout droit	straight ahead		
tout le monde	everyone, everybody	**Y**	
tout(e) seul(e)	all alone		
le train	train	y	there
tranquille	quiet, calm		
le travail (travaux)	work		
travailler	to work		
la traversée	crossing		
traverser	to cross		
très	very		
le trésor	treasure		
troisième	third		
la trompette	trumpet		

Internet links

If you have access to the Internet, there are lots of useful Web sites you can visit to help you improve your French. Throughout this book, we have recommended Web sites where you can practice your French and improve your language skills. To access these sites, go to the Usborne Quicklinks Web site at **www.usborne-quicklinks.com** and type in the key words "easy french".

Why use the Internet?

The Internet is a great resource for language learning. On the sites mentioned in this book, you can listen to French being spoken, test your language skills with interactive puzzles and read more about how the language works. Here are some examples of the kinds of Web sites that we have recommended:

• a Web site where you can practice different French grammar points through interactive games, including matching the pairs, mini quizzes and wordsearches.

• a Web site where you can read and listen to French expressions, and learn more about French grammar rules.

• a Web site where you can test your French by filling the gaps in a selection of French sentences.

• a Web site where you can test your French with some illustrated exercises on everyday words.

For links to these and other exciting French Web sites, go to **www.usborne-quicklinks.com** and type in the key words "easy french".

Listening to languages

On many language sites, you can listen to recordings of someone speaking the language. To hear these recordings, you need a sound card in your computer (many computers have sound cards already installed). You also need some other programs, called "plug-ins", such as Windows® Media Player or RealPlayer®. You may already have these on your computer. If not, you can download them for free from the Internet.

Downloadable puzzles

In Usborne Quicklinks, you will also find a selection of Usborne picture puzzles that you can use to practice your French. Print out the puzzles and fill them in, then go back to Usborne Quicklinks to check your answers. Each puzzle has its own set of clues to help you.

Windows® is a trademark of Microsoft Corporation, registered in the US and other countries. RealPlayer® is a trademark of RealNetworks, Inc., registered in the US and other countries.

Site availability

The links in Usborne Quicklinks are regularly reviewed and updated, but occasionally you may get a message that a site is unavailable. This may be temporary, so try again later, or even the next day. If any of the recommended sites close down, we will, if possible, replace them with suitable alternatives, so you will always find an up-to-date list of sites in Usborne Quicklinks.

Computer not essential

Don't worry if you don't have access to the Internet. On its own this book is a complete and fun guide to learning French.

Extras

Here are some other plug-ins that you may need to enable your browser to display videos, animations or interactive games:

• QuickTime - enables you to view video clips.

• Flash™ - lets you play animations.

• Shockwave® - lets you play animations and interactive programs.

Web sites that use plug-ins usually have a link to click on to download the plug-in you need. Although the download can take some time, you only have to do it once, and it gives you full access to some really good sites. For more information about plug-ins, go to **www.usborne-quicklinks.com** and click on **Net Help**.

QuickTime is a trademark of Apple Computer, Inc., registered in the US and other countries.
Flash™ and Shockwave® are trademarks of Macromedia®, registered in the US and other countries.

Index

Acknowledgements

Cover: Macduff Everton/CORBIS;
p.12 sunset, car/Digital Vision; **p.13** coastline/Digital
Vision; **p.21** teenagers/Digital Vision; **p.25** Gail
Mooner/CORBIS; **p.29** women shopping/Digital Vision;
p.33 Owen Franken/CORBIS; **p.37** girls
chatting/CORBIS; **p.41** world map, beach scene/Digital
Vision; **p.49** skiers/CORBIS; **p.57** Hulton-Deutsch
Collection x2/CORBIS; **p.61** Owen Franken/CORBIS;
p.65 boys talking/Digital Vision;
p.69 Fotografica/CORBIS; **p.73** Neil Beer/CORBIS;
p.77 North American Scene/Digital Vision; **p.82** three
children/Digital Vision; **p.83** Michael T. Sedan/CORBIS;
p.87 Joseph Sohm/CORBIS and astronaut/Digital Vision;
p.91 Jean-Pierre Lescourret/CORBIS and Michael
Prince/CORBIS; **p.95** Stuart Westmorland/CORBIS;
p.124 man with headphones/Powerstock Zefa;
p.125 Kevin Fleming/CORBIS

First published in 2002 by Usborne Publishing Ltd,
83-85 Saffron Hill, London EC1N 8RT, England.
www.usborne.com
First published in America in 2002.
Copyright © 2002, 1992 Usborne Publishing Ltd. AE

Some of the material in this book was originally
published in *Learn French*.

The name Usborne and the devices 🔔 🌐 are Trade Marks of Usborne Publishing Ltd.
All rights reserved. No part of this
publication may be reproduced, stored in a retrieval system, or
transmitted in any form or by any means, electronic, mechanical,
photocopying, recording or otherwise, without the prior
permission of the publisher.

Printed in Italy.

Usborne Publishing is not responsible and does not accept liability for the availability or
content of any Web site other than its own, or for any exposure to harmful, offensive, or
inaccurate material which may appear on the Web. Usborne Publishing will have no liability
for any damage or loss caused by viruses that may be downloaded as a result of browsing
the sites it recommends.